T0079714

SALMON

Edible

Series Editor: Andrew F. Smith

EDIBLE is a revolutionary new series of books dedicated to food and drink that explores the rich history of cuisine. Each book reveals the global history and culture of one type of food or beverage.

Already published

Apple Erika Janik *Beef* Lorna Piatti-Farnell *Bread* William Rubel *Cake* Nicola Humble *Caviar* Nichola Fletcher *Champagne* Becky Sue Epstein *Cheese* Andrew Dalby *Chocolate* Sarah Moss and Alexander Badenoch *Cocktails* Joseph M. Carlin *Curry* Colleen Taylor Sen *Dates* Nawal Nasrallah *Game* Paula Young Lee *Gin* Lesley Jacobs Solmonson *Hamburger* Andrew F. Smith *Herbs* Gary Allen *Hot Dog* Bruce Kraig *Ice Cream* Laura B. Weiss *Lemon* Toby Sonneman *Lobster* Elisabeth Townsend *Milk* Hannah Velten *Mushroom* Cynthia D. Bertelsen *Offal* Nina Edwards *Olive* Fabrizia Lanza *Oranges* Clarissa Hyman *Pancake* Ken Albala *Pie* Janet Clarkson *Pineapple* Kaori O'Connor *Pizza* Carol Helstosky *Pork* Katharine M. Rogers *Potato* Andrew F. Smith *Rum* Richard Foss *Salmon* Nicolaas Mink *Sandwich* Bee Wilson *Soup* Janet Clarkson *Spices* Fred Czarra *Tea* Helen Saberi *Whiskey* Kevin R. Kosar *Wine* Marc Millon

Salmon

A Global History

Nicolaas Mink

REAKTION BOOKS

To Mom and Dad, teachers of wanderlust

Published by Reaktion Books Ltd
33 Great Sutton Street
London EC1V 0DX, UK
www.reaktionbooks.co.uk

First published 2013

Copyright © Nicolaas Mink 2013

Printed and bound in China
by Toppan Printing Co. Ltd.

A catalogue record for this book is available from the British Library

ISBN 978 1 78023 183 9

Contents

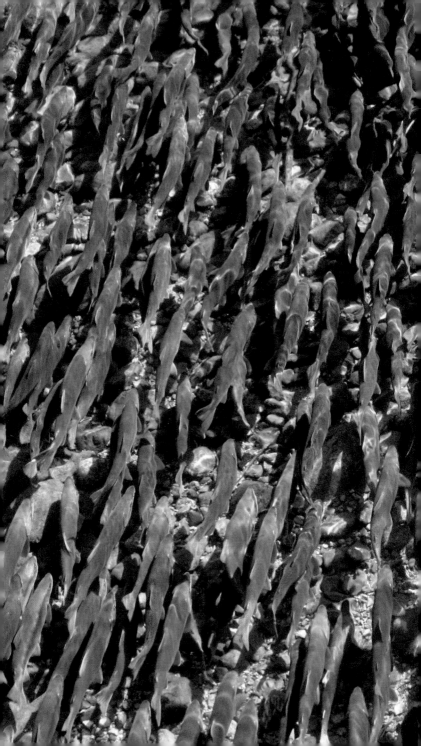

Prologue: Looking Back from Sitka, Alaska

The whole of nature is a conjugation of the verb to eat.

William Ralph Inge

From above, Sitka appears to be little more than a frontier outpost tucked secretly among the thousands of islands that make up the Alexander Archipelago of the Alaskan panhandle. It is a harsh, remote and unforgiving little place, a community on the edge. The vast and endless expanse of the Pacific Ocean bounds Sitka to the west, while impossibly rugged peaks crowned by ice sheets straddle the village to the east. Between ocean and ice, spruce, hemlock and muskeg tremble under the weight of the persistent downpours, revealing that this landscape, so hostile and foreboding, is home to the world's last great remaining chunk of temperate rainforest.

But visit Sitka in the summer and autumn, and you notice a biotic event that dwarfs even the region's towering old-growth trees: the annual salmon runs. Every year, salmon pulse and course up rivers and streams by the millions, seized by a desire to return to their place of birth, where they spawn before returning their bodies to the gravel and soil that nurtured them as juveniles years before. Every year, more salmon return to the borough of Sitka to spawn than now exist in the wild in the entire Atlantic Ocean. In a good spawning year, salmon outnumber humans several thousand to one.

I came to find this out when I moved from the fertile prairies of the American Midwest to Sitka a few years back. Living in Sitka, you come to understand that salmon define everything about this place, from its forests and streams to its culture and economy. Salmon *are* Sitka, the sovereigns of our ecosystems, economy, culture, history and, of course, our diet. It has been that way for at least eight millennia, since the final glacier retreated from the outer coasts of Southeast Alaska, and Mount Edgecombe, a now-dormant volcano, covered the entire region with a 3½ m (12 ft) blanket of ash at the end of the last ice age. Shortly after that, salmon recolonized the land, the streams and the forests, and humans followed soon behind.

Three thousand years ago, Sitka's earliest human residents had already begun to use elaborate and sophisticated salmon-catching technologies, from fish weirs, fish traps and gaff

Grilled king salmon, caught off the coast of Sitka, Alaska, served with a locally harvested salmonberry salad.

Sitka waterfront, Alaska, late 19th century.

hooks to spears, and with these innovations salmon became the region's primary food – smoked, dried, salted, fresh or fermented. The Tlingit, later inhabitants of the region, built their gastronomic worlds on salmon, too. Between June and December, the Tlingit maximized their salmon harvest by establishing mobile fish camps at Redoubt Bay, Indian River and Starrigavan Creek, a cultural and culinary system that provided a seven-month salmon harvest in good years. Sockeye salmon pulsed up Redoubt Bay in June and July; pink and chum salmon ran up Indian River in August and September; and silver salmon finished the Tlingit's annual salmon feast at Starrigavan, running up that watershed until the winter solstice, the latest single salmon run in the region.

In the late eighteenth century, Europeans began to skirt the west coast of the North Pacific, and it was abundant salmon that provided crew members of British, Russian and French ships with their first fresh food in months. In 1804, Russian settlers destroyed the Tlingit village at Sitka, and took the salmon for their own. 'Aside from bread', quipped one

Sitka residents overlooking spawning salmon in the Indian River during the late 19th century.

Russian trader in Sitka, 'fish represents the chief food' of the townspeople. Salmon were so numerous that the Russian American Company provided 'fresh fish from the Company without cost . . . [when] the fish are running', while 'the rest of the year salt fish is also given out free'. The Russians relished salmon in ways similar to the Tlingit. *Yukola*, a type of dried salmon passed along to the Russians by the Aleuts, became the staple food for colonists. Many called it 'Kamchatka bread', referring to the name of the peninsula on Russia's east coast between the Sea of Okhotsk and the Pacific Ocean. Like most European colonists, the Russians exported what they could not eat. By the 1810s, Sitka's salmon supported the first European commercial fishery on the west coast of North America. By the end of that decade, the Russian nobility in St Petersburg and Moscow were dining on salmon from Sitka Sound.

In 1867, the United States took possession of Alaska in a ceremony overlooking spawning salmon in Sitka Sound. In 1878, the Cutting Packing Company opened the first cannery in Sitka, the second in all of Alaska. It existed for only two years, but during its life it shipped 10,000 cases of salmon to all corners of the globe. Before long, the much larger Pyramid Packing Company, makers of Pharaoh brand canned salmon, replaced Cutting. Salmon was becoming an industrial food around the world, and in Sitka these canneries ignited a new, industrialized salmon economy, attracting workers from Mexico, Russia, America, the Philippines and China. Dozens of nationalities flooded Sitka, all to participate, in some small measure, in the emerging global salmon economy based in this small fishing town.

Today, the city remains one of the North Pacific's great salmon entrepots. It is a city built on fish. Three large processing plants and half-a-dozen smaller ones annually ship about 25 million lb (11.4 million kg) of wild salmon from Sitka to every corner of the globe. That, it turns out, is about one in

A salmon troller fishing the waters off Sitka.

every twenty wild salmon consumed around the world. In 2011, Southeast Alaska's production outpaced Southwest Alaska's storied Bristol Bay salmon fishery, making it the world's great salmon producer. Here, surrounded by the productive watersheds of the Tongass National Forest to the west and the upwelling from the continental shelf to the east, salmon transform from nature to culture, from a local natural resource to a global food.

Of course, turning a product of nature into something edible for humans relies heavily on the technological instruments, folklore and rituals that make up the toolkit of human culture. I learned this much on my first fishing trip out of Sitka. On one stunningly beautiful June day, my friend Scott and I landed three king salmon, all radiant in the reflection of a rare morning sun. Back on shore, Scott filleted each fish, while I bagged up what modern Americans consider to be waste, even though the heads, bones, eggs and eyes that will find their way into our compost piles and refuse bins have made – and continue to make – perfectly desirable food for many millions, including certain people here in Sitka. (I have, incidentally, heard the eyeballs described as luscious and melt-in-your-mouth.) Shunning the eyeballs, we completed our ritual not much after noon, and I took home a side from each fish – stunningly perfect fillets ranging in colour from blood-red to coral, all of them layered with cream-coloured fat typical of a bright, ocean-run king salmon. Longtime Sitka fisherman Eric Jordan calls these king fillets the 'the tastiest, the sweetest, and richest . . . around', and it is hard not to agree.

For the next week we gorged on nature's bounty: salmon seared in olive oil, topped with mustard crème fraîche and lentils, a take on a classic French preparation; salt and pepper baked salmon, crowned with white truffle butter and plated with broiled asparagus; lemon-grilled salmon with dill aioli,

Seared king salmon with mustard crème fraîche and lentils.

broccoli and new potatoes. Curried salmon salad followed right behind, and we ended our week with a cast-iron pot of salmon chowder, served with a crunchy baguette. Each one of these dishes revealed an intermingling of our globalized food culture and the local ecology of a tiny place on the North Pacific. At the same time, it is hard not to imagine that our use of salmon mirrors much of what has been going on here for millennia, minus, perhaps, the truffle oil. Our week-long feast complete, I borrowed a friend's vacuum sealer, loaded the plastic-covered fish into a worn-out Nissan pickup and headed for a local processing plant, where we jury-rigged a blast freezer out of the plant's bait sheds. The remaining salmon would now last the winter in my freezer.

Given the heightened interest in the study of food in popular and academic circles, I am often struck by how little discussion takes place about the last step in my salmon binge, perhaps the most important part of any food in any culture: preservation. It is the hidden link in our food chain, and my mastery of preservation technology – both in my domestic refrigerator and in the fish processor's bait shed – allowed me to manipulate nature's decay just enough to ensure that the fish would remain food for my friends and family, instead of for the bugs, eagles or bears, whose palates are more amenable to rot and the chemicals it triggers in our brains once the decomposing flesh encounters our senses. In many ways, food *is* preservation. Take a look inside a modern supermarket: it is not only a showplace of food, but also an emporium showcasing the various ways in which humans store food before it is consumed. Humans, you might have noticed, do some pretty interesting things to preserve food – we spray it with chemicals in the case of many supermarket-bought grapes, and we construct elaborate heat-removing machines in the case of frozen peas and ice cream. In turn, food actually becomes our preservation techniques. So it is with salmon, one of the world's great foods.

My argument in *Salmon: A Global History* – and the scaffolding on which the book is built – is that salmon-as-food and salmon-as-preservation-technology are synonymous. Much of what global consumers have known and continue to know about salmon (as well as many of the ways they have used the fish in their diets) stems from prevailing regimes of preservation. On salmon-producing coasts, fresh salmon abounds for several months a year, but people have used various methods of preservation to extend the palatability, edibility and geographic range of the consumption of salmon and, at the same time, to remake the fish into a new kind of food. For most of human history, preserving salmon for food and trade turned to the use of salt, smoke, controlled fermentation, drying and, to a lesser extent, acid. These technological solutions to seasonal abundance and scarcity merged human culture with salmon's nature to create foods as different

Freshly caught pink salmon, now famous for travelling the world; mostly in a can.

as Scandinavian gravlax and Scottish kippered fish – part salmon flesh, part human innovation, all food.

Beginning in the 1880s, however, canning – largely along the coasts of Japan, Russia and Alaska – eclipsed these older forms of preservation, simultaneously making salmon available to consumers worldwide and producing a certain type of cooked food characterized by a long shelf life and mild flavour. Once salmon hit the can, the pungent odours of alder, peat or cedar smoke faded into the culinary past, as did the salt, sugar and pepper. As it was for millions of others, canned salmon was the salmon of my youth. I hardly knew that fresh or smoked salmon existed until I went to college. One of my earliest recollections of visiting my maternal grandmother in rural Illinois in the American Midwest is of her salmon patties, an odd combination of eggs, ketchup, Saltine crackers and canned Alaskan salmon whisked together and fried in dollops of butter in one of those old frontier cast-iron pans that make it appear as if food is spiralling towards a celestial black hole. I remember the dish as one of the staples of my grandparents'

An assortment of salmon, just plucked from a subsistence gillnet.

household, a food rivalled only by my grandmother's pickled beets, beef stew and apple pie.

Since the 1980s, however, a new form of salmon has found its way from streams and oceans to homes and restaurants: fresh salmon. People on the coasts, of course, have been eating salmon straight from the adjacent waters since time immemorial, but under a new preservation regime that fea improved distribution networks, novel salmon-rearing te niques and innovative developments in the cold chain, a fresh market developed on a global scale. This new system allowed greater access to raw salmon. In the process, salmon became a new, malleable food that remade the cooking and eating of the fish. The number of fresh salmon recipes exploded in cookbooks as this new form of salmon entered supermarkets at prices comparable to, and sometimes cheaper than, those of beef and pork. Consumers, too, substituted this new food for declining stocks of whitefish like cod and haddock. A new food and foodway was born, one made of the same raw material, but only vaguely resembling the flaky pink substance found in a can.

Salmon make up about 12 per cent of the world's fish consumption, and Sitka just might be the perfect place in which to begin a story about salmon. The city's past causes us to reflect upon the ways in which people have turned salmon into food and, in turn, how these inimitable creatures have coursed through human history and remade global foodways in the process. However, first we must turn to nature's food web, for that is where the story of this charismatic fish and ever-changing food begins.

I

A Natural History of Salmon Eating

It leaves its native river at an early stage of growth, and going,
even naturalists know not where, returns of ample size and
nourishment, exposing itself in the narrowest streams, as if
Nature intended it as a special boon to man.

Cassell's Dictionary of Cookery

One of the world's great gastronomic events occurred about
25 million years ago, millennia before humanity's ancestors
sprang from the plains of Africa to conquer the globe. It was
then, sandwiched between the Oligocene and Miocene epochs,
that a few errant fish spilled forth from their freshwater
homes and into an awaiting ocean in search of food that
seemed to be increasingly scarce in their freshwater environments. Scientists speculate that colder temperatures associated
with the Miocene epoch decreased the carrying capacity of
temperate freshwater environments while simultaneously boost-
ing the food produced by adjacent oceans, largely due to
increased upwelling.

These fish were pioneers, and they soon colonized the
oceans and rivers of the northern hemisphere. About twenty
million years ago, they pushed past the divide between the
Atlantic and the Pacific, creating two separate genera – *Salmo*

and *Onchorynchus* – that each evolved with the ecologies of their respective oceans and watersheds. These fish weathered scores of the Earth's warming and cooling periods, glaciations, floods, droughts and volcanic activity, soon becoming the most abundant epipelagic, or near-surface, fish north of the equator. In the process, salmon emerged as an integral part of nature's complex food web, a keystone species both on land and in the ocean. Over time, these climatic, geologic and environmental events imprinted themselves on the bodies of the fish themselves. Six hundred thousand years ago, the modern salmon was born.

Those of us who have welcomed salmon into our cultures and our homes, and onto our dinner tables, usually do not ruminate much on the evolutionary or natural history of the foods that we put on our plates. Food, after all, occupies the present, especially in the world of modern convenience stores and fast food. Our distribution and manufacturing

Purse seiner *Cloud Nine* returning from a day of fishing in the North Pacific.

systems now operate at such dizzying speeds that in the time it takes for us to enjoy dinner, food can be transported across entire continents. This means that food is always in the here and now; it is everywhere and nowhere. Yet every time people eat the pliant flesh of salmon they are tasting evolution, natural history and deep time. Indeed, salmon's evolutionary, natural and life histories turned what might have otherwise been a common fish into one of the handful of most important sources of marine-derived fats and proteins the world has ever known. These long and complicated histories still reveal themselves in the ways cultures across the globe cook and eat salmon. Every taste, every bite, conveys an elaborate alchemy within the nature, culture and history of this fish.

So what, exactly, is a salmon? The question seems simple enough, but its answer leads us to some surprising and unexpected places. Ecologically, salmon inhabit large swathes of the North Pacific and Atlantic Oceans and, thanks to their introduction in the late nineteenth century by fish culturists, the South Pacific and South Atlantic as well. For eaters, salmon are usually one of seven species from the *Onchorynchus* and *Salmo* genera that English speakers call king, keta, pink, coho, sockeye, masu and Atlantic salmon. The culinary lingua franca of salmon, however, contains plenty of synonyms and regional and national variations. In many parts of the globe, king salmon are called tyee, Chinook, black mouth and chub. Sockeye go by the names red, blueback, nerka and Kokanee; coho can also be called bluebacks, though they are more often described as silverside, white or silver salmon; to many, keta is simply a marketing term for less pleasing sobriquets like chum, chub and dog; masu is cherry salmon; pinks are humpbacks; and Atlantic salmon has dozens of names, depending on when and where it was caught.

At the same time, salmon nomenclature is actually more complicated than these regional and national variations, for the names we give salmon – and the very idea of salmon themselves – are as much gastronomic as ecological. The Salmonidae family contains six genera and 150 species, yet we know only seven species as salmon. Many of the other 143 species have as much scientific right to the salmon moniker as the seven species that eaters call salmon. Part of the Salmonidae genus, *Salvelinus*, is to all intents and purposes a salmon. Species in this genus are often anadromous (spending most of their lives in the sea but returning to fresh water to spawn) and they exhibit many of the same physiological traits and evolutionary histories as those possessed by the fish consumers call salmon. However, *Salvelinus* often find themselves in fishermens' nets and on eaters' plates under the names Arctic char, brook trout, lake trout or Dolly Varden. There are even plenty of *Salmo* and *Onchorynchus* that leap into our pans, but not as salmon. *Salmo trutta* is the Atlantic salmon's closest living relative. Genetically it is more similar to the Atlantic salmon than pink salmon is to king salmon. Eaters, however, call it a brook trout. Most perplexingly of all, scientists studying salmon DNA in the 1980s concluded that rainbow trout were more closely related to king and coho salmon than king and coho were to keta, pink or sockeye. These scientists cleaved the very category of salmon in two.

As muddled and complex as it might be, salmon nonetheless do have a nature – a set of qualities that distinguish them from their piscine cousins. For the humans who wait on shore with nets or patrol the coasts with hooks, the most remarkable – some might say miraculous – part of a salmon's nature is its ability to transform the sun's energy into food for humans more quickly and efficiently than

Sockeye fishermen, British Columbia, late 19th century.

almost any other creature in the sea. In nature's food web, salmon promise tremendous returns for people who rely on turning the sun's heat into the chemical energy that human digestive systems then cycle through our bodies. Salmon so efficiently convert the sun's energy into food because they are dietary generalists. Much like us, they eat everything. They do not have special features like a whale's baleen or a

dolphin's canines that might restrict their diets. In fa...
salmon are constantly feeding, in large part because of ther...
gill-rakers, which continually filter food from the ocean.
Salmon passively consume daphnia, diaptomus and cyclops
(all zooplankton), surface plankton, small crustaceans and
dozens of larvae in such a way. They also actively eat squid,
candlefish, herring and sand lance. They thus feed on several
different trophic levels and in a variety of different ways.
When this characteristic is combined with their extraordinary
metabolic and growth rates, a normal fish becomes an
extraordinary producer of proteins and fats, which, sometime in the not too distant past, exploded from a chain
reaction in the sun.

Not only do salmon efficiently convert the sun's energy
into food for humans, but they also deliver that food in
meal-sized packages right into the hands, hooks and nets
of waiting humans. The survival mechanism that first
caused salmon to stray from their natal streams 25 million
years ago today yields this unique trait. Scientists call it
anadromy, and it sends every salmon on a journey from its
freshwater home to the ocean and back during its lifetime.
There are 20,000 species of fish in the oceans, but as luck
turns out, only 87 types are anadromous. Their fellow
anadromous cousins include shad, striped bass, lampreys,
sturgeon and smelt. (Eels, in case you are wondering, are
catadromous, moving from salt water to fresh water, then
to salt water again to spawn.) The anadromous impulse
sends salmon born in British Columbia's Fraser River
coursing towards the Alaska Current, across the Bering Sea
and along the Bering Sea Gyre, after which they ride the
Subarctic Current back to the North American coast.
Anadromy convinces salmon born on Russia's Kamchatka
Peninsula to cruise with the Okhotsk Sea Gyre and the

st Kamchatka, Kuroshio and Oyashio Currents to the Bering Sea, where they live their adult lives, before riding the Alaska Current back to their home streams. Anadromy, too, entices salmon from Iceland to swim east to the Faroes and the Norwegian and Irminger Seas, before they return to their homes. Both Atlantic and Pacific salmon sweep, spin and dart across vast stretches of ocean, many travelling in loops that tie together thousands of miles of these waterways. Finally, guided by smell, taste, light and even the Earth's magnetic field, the fish return to their natal streams to spawn. There, their bodies deposit the ocean's nutrients in the forests and streams that gave them life – or, if we are lucky enough, they deposit these nutrients into our bodies.

Salmon's anadromous life cycle is one of the miracles of the human food system. It accounts for how eaters have historically accessed and used salmon in their diets. This life cycle sweeps all salmon through the ocean, where they gather the ocean's energy, only then to sacrifice it to the plants and animals on land. Most animals in the human culinary repertoire exploit relatively small areas to provide people with food; this is especially the case in animals farmed in factories, which have little choice but to stay put and have their food come to them. Salmon, however, gather energy from areas so large that until just a few decades ago their life histories were largely a mystery. Moreover, because salmon return to their natal streams in a relatively short span of time – usually most of the cohort arrives in a period of several weeks – this process produces nutrient-rich foods in astounding density. Anadromy, in a funny way, produced nature's original convenience food: calorically dense and reliably delivered straight to people's homes in such vast quantities that it seemed limitless. Salmon runs in major rivers and streams placed hundreds of billions of usable calories in the hands of cultures that the fish almost single-handedly supported.

However, salmon's life cycle, evolution and natural history do more than just create an efficient delivery vehicle for proteins and fats for waiting humans. They also combine to form the very taste of this food. Taste and place, of course, have co-evolved into a vibrant whole that renders food intelligible to palates and souls. The French call this *goût de terroir* (taste of the earth); English-speakers call it the taste of the place. The same could be said about the interweaving of time and history, both over a food's own life and over the evolutionary life of an entire species.

Few creatures that we call food demonstrate the taste of time, history and evolution better than salmon. Pink salmon, *Onchorynchus gorbuscha,* evolved over millions of years to inhabit the smallest streams that spill into the North Pacific. They are the smallest salmon and most of their freshwater habitat extends only a few miles inland. Their final runs back to their birthplaces to spawn are marked by short trips up shallow rivers. It is a rare occurrence to witness a pink salmon more than a few dozen miles from the ocean's shore.

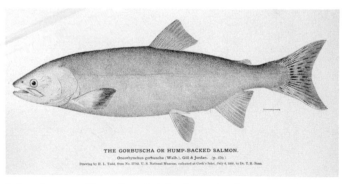

THE GORBUSCHA OR HUMP-BACKED SALMON.
Oncorhynchus gorbuscha (Walb.), Gill & Jordan. (p. 470.)
Drawing by H. L. Todd, from No. 27742, U. S. National Museum, collected at Cook's Inlet, July 8, 1880, by Dr. T. H. Bean.

Late 19th-century illustration of pink salmon, then known as gorbuscha or the humpbacked salmon.

The flesh of pink salmon, in turn, reflects these shorter runs; their bodies store little fat and their muscles do not develop in the same ways as those of salmon that need to make longer freshwater journeys. Eaters experience this natural history as soft flesh with a light flake. With little fat and less developed muscle, the taste of pink salmon exhibits little of that luxuriant depth – the umami, some eaters call it – that many associate with higher-value salmon from the Atlantic and Pacific Oceans. This life cycle reveals itself as a taste that some might mistake for that of a delicate trout, a subtle reminder of the blurred boundaries in our gastronomic taxonomies.

On the other hand, king salmon display an entirely different combination of evolution and taste. The largest of the globe's salmon species – at least since the last sabretooth salmon became extinct 2 million years ago – king salmon have evolved with the Northern Hemisphere's longest, most powerful waterways. Rivers such as the Amur, MacKenzie, Yukon and Sacramento pulse through their bodies, and you can taste this power in their flesh. Their muscles grow large, dense and tight as proteins bond with one another in ways that allow them to make their monumental journeys of hundreds if not thousands of miles. They, too, must harvest enough of the sun's energy to make this journey, which they store as fat, our nearest star's most concentrated chemical form in the animal body. King salmon have a greater portion of fat to lean than any other salmon species, and the longer the journey home, the more fat they store. These voluptuous fats are unleashed on the tongue, providing a counterpoint to a dense flesh with a texture that sometimes resembles that of braised pork. Indeed, the bellies of smoked ocean-caught king salmon bear a striking similarity to American-style bacon. Because of

A single king salmon, the largest and fattiest of the globe's salmon species, thanks to its evolution with the globe's largest river system.

the king's evolution in highly specialized environments, it has a relatively small habitat and is therefore the rarest of salmon species. King salmon account for less than 0.1 per cent of the globe's salmon. Prized by wealthy consumers, this scarcity maps itself onto taste buds, making king salmon an elite food. Unexpectedly, perhaps, evolution is even refracted through our marketplaces and our class structures.

Between these two poles sit keta, masu, coho and Atlantic salmon, all biological and ecological generalists. They have evolved to inhabit a variety of freshwater ecosystems, so their taste and texture, more than those of other species, reflect the habitats of each subpopulation. One of the unique aspects of a salmon's natural history stems from the fact that while hundreds of millions of salmon mingle together in the Atlantic and Pacific Oceans, they nonetheless almost all return to the spot where their ancestors spawned. They have incredible fidelity, in other words, to their natal streams. This not only creates distinct and isolated

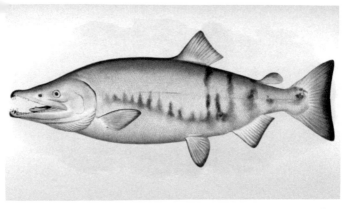

'Dog Salmon, Breeding Male', illustration, 1906. For obvious reasons, dog salmon are sold under the more palatable name of keta salmon.

genetic subpopulations among species (scientists call these demes), but also profoundly affects the tastes, texture and body composition within each species, especially among species like keta, coho, masu and Atlantic salmon, which have adapted to a variety of different environments. An experienced fish broker can tell by sight and taste the difference between an Atlantic salmon whose ancestors stalked the Loire River and one that dwelled in the Thames. Coho flesh can be soft and rich or firm and mild, depending on its spawning river system. Very often, keta reared in short coastal streams yield soft flesh, resembling that of pink salmon, with a flavour that one might describe as earthy, even musty at times. This flavour stems from the keta's favourite food: jellyfish and smaller gelatinous zooplankton, which make up more than half its diet. By contrast, the flavour of keta from one of the world's largest extant freshwater salmon habitats, the Yukon River, resembles more an elite king's than a humble pink's. I have a fisherman friend who swears that not even the most discerning gourmand can tell the difference between a Yukon River keta and a king caught from a smaller river system.

Sockeye have perhaps the most unique evolutionary history of all salmon, contributing not only to a taste that is undoubtedly the richest of all salmon flavours, but to a characteristic deep red flesh. The heart of sockeye country is situated between Russia's Sea of Okhotsk and Alaska's Bristol Bay, and unlike all other salmon, sockeyes spend much of their lives in lakes. Before heading to sea, most of them spend the first two years of their lives living in fresh-water lakes where they feed on series of microscopic crustaceans and zooplankton, which leads to a lifelong commitment to eating lower on the food chain than do other salmon. Throughout their adult lives in the ocean, sockeyes continue to feed on tiny zooplankton and other little crustaceans, which provide greater doses of a carotenoid called astaxanthin than those found in salmon that feed on fish, squid and jellyfish higher up on the food chain. The bright, dense, rich flesh that sockeyes so often exhibit stems from these feeding patterns and their place in the food chain.

Within all of these species, of course, there still exist tremendous variations in taste, colour and texture. Each season produces new tastes, much like a wine from, say, Burgundy does. For most of their natural history, salmon have been wild foods, so their taste, texture and colour resist the homogeneity demanded by industrial food production. Every single wild salmon is different. This is part of the gastronomic beauty of the fish, even though it frustrates consumers with palates trained by corporate food to expect conformity. This fact, too, has been written by evolution and the currents of deep time, processes that privilege diversity over uniformity, chaos over control.

Although salmon symbolize some of our most powerful images of the natural world, they are not just natural, wild beings, of course. Like all foods, they represent a tango between nature and culture, ocean and plate.

2
Cured

The Salmon is accounted the King of freshwater fish.

Izaak Walton

To the Yurok tribe that inhabited the land along the Klamath River next to the Pacific Ocean, salmon were far more than a part of nature and far more than a simple fish. To them, salmon were an idea and a thing that transcended time, place and culture. Erik Erikson, a University of California anthropologist, spent months with the tribe in the early 1930s. He marvelled at their stories about panthers, eagles, buzzards and dozens of other creatures that made the Mediterranean environment along the Pacific Coast their home. The Yurok related these animals to their homes and constructed their sense of place with them.

Salmon were another matter, however. 'I just asked for a fable about this animal', he later wrote. Unfortunately for Erikson, salmon were 'the food itself', and no stories could be made up about them. Salmon's importance as food to the Yurok pushed them beyond the mere realm of storytelling. Salmon were existence incarnate, and the repetition of any words about them represented not a story but 'a kind of prayer, an assurance that values are durable and immovable'.

Native American fishermen repairing their nets, Celilo Falls, Oregon, 1950.

Transforming a charismatic animal into 'the food itself', something hundreds of cultures did (and continue to do) across the globe, required more than just a remarkable animal set against a backdrop of an ever-changing natural world and evolutionary history. It required a set of rituals to turn this animal into food. We confront these rituals every time we pray before a meal, place our knives beside our forks or choose to drape a piece of meat over an open flame rather than drop it into a pot of boiling water. For the Yurok, salmon rituals involved abstaining from storytelling, following elaborate rules about what men and women could and could not do with salmon, and constructing and using fish-catching technologies that were linked closely to the religious and social rules of the tribe.

The most elaborate rituals took place once the salmon left the water. These are the cultural worlds of food processing, which, as anthropologists tell us, take two forms. Processing for immediate use takes the form of cooking; processing for future consumption takes the form of preservation. Salmon's abundance in space and time precludes its immediate use by humans, and due to its rich, oily flesh, rot – the recycling of nutrients so that they may return to the earth – takes hold almost immediately, reminding us that humans are not the only things that need nourishment. In salmon killed with full stomachs, significant decomposition of the flesh can begin after about ten minutes. In some conditions, within an hour a fish can be commercially and, sometimes, gastronomically useless. Thus the vast majority of salmon must go through some form of preservation for later human consumption, even if it only involves putting fish on ice.

Before industrialization radically rewrote and reconfigured the global food system, cultures across the globe relied on elaborate preservation schemes that chemically and physically altered the nature of salmon so that it could be stored for later use. Given the diversity of the experience with salmon as food, it is impossible to explore fully the myriad ways that the globe's peoples took salmon and made it a storable food, then used that product in their culinary repertoires. However, a quick world tour, if you will, reveals the depth of salmon's importance as a preserved substance and the breadth of ways it was used. Preserving salmon was a necessity born of abundance, and one that hoped to ward off that dreaded condition of scarcity by eliminating the boom and bust food cycles that the uncertainties of seasonality, climate, weather and, of course, salmon's very own natural history brought to people who built their lives, cultures and diets around this food.

Scientifically, preservation is actually a process called denaturation, and it is at the heart of most types of food storage. The application of heat, smoke and salt physically and chemically changes (or denatures) foods, specifically proteins, so that spoilage is either controlled or minimized. Salting, for instance, works on a simple premise. When salt is first applied to salmon, it draws water out of the semi-permeable cell walls. Osmosis seeks a state of equilibrium, so some of that water then returns back to the cells, only this time with a dose of the salt. That salt coagulates the salmon's protein, making it less hospitable to the bacteria that begin nature's rot. Creating salty cells is the key to curing salmon, and for thousands of years,

Freshly smoked sockeye salmon in a brown sugar brine.

A Native American spearing salmon below a falls, California, *c.* 1880.

as Mark Kurlansky's *Salt* points out, this method represented one of the primary ways of preserving food. In addition to having an antimicrobial effect, the application of smoke, like heat, removes water from cells, which often act as a breeding ground for the bacteria. Curing therefore halts one of the key processes of death: decomposition. In a world in which the cold chain and cans have come to dominate all forms of food preservation, it is remarkable to consider the divergent, diverse and, often, creative ways in which people re-engineered the nature of salmon for later use after the great annual runs of the fish dried to a trickle.

Take the peoples of the Pacific Rim. For the Tlingit of what would become British Columbia and Alaska, salmon straddled a unique place between food and wealth. They were both of these things – a commodity and a taste, a symbol of exchange and a centrepiece of their culinary culture. The

A variety of different modern preparations of the ancient classic: smoked salmon.

abundance of salmon was so great on the land and waters surrounded by the temperate rainforests of the region that preservation took many forms and had many styles, creating a series of unique salmon foods for the people who lived there.

Like many native peoples of North America, the Tlingit eschewed the heavy salting that other cultures embraced as a way to preserve salmon; instead they constructed *atx'aan hidi*, or smoke houses, which allowed them to preserve both salmon and halibut. *Náa yadi* was salmon preserved with a light smoke; other salmon were dried and stored for later use. *Chil xook* was one of the most popular types of preserved salmon. It could be made out of smoked or fresh salmon, but regardless of the initial raw material, the Tlingit left the fish out first to air dry, then to freeze. The three-part preservation process, from smoked to dried to frozen, imparted a unique taste to the fish, and helped it to last throughout the winter. Dipped in the rich oil of rendered candlefish, a sort of pre-modern dipping sauce that mellowed the rough edges of the preserved fish, *chil xook* was a favourite food of pre-contact Tlingit.

Further south, the Yurok and other salmon eaters along the Klamath River smoked salmon and layered it in large baskets between leaves from pepperwood trees, which imparted flavour to the fish and protected it from moths. When the Yurok were ready to consume the fish they paired it with a bread or mush, called *ka-go*, made from acorns gathered in late autumn. 'It is very nutritious and gives great power of endurance', recalled one. During spiritual fasts, priests were allowed only one meal a day of this smoked salmon and *ka-go*. The Alsea, a coastal people in what would become the present-day state of Oregon, smoked and sun dried their salmon, a technique, one anthropologist wrote, that 'permitted a winter of leisure unknown to any people lacking a plentiful and easily preserved food source'. The Alsea reconstituted the dried salmon in boiling water and, if they were lucky, dipped it in bowls of whale oil.

Surely the most ingenious way of storing salmon for later use in this part of North America was through the making of something the Wintu-speaking people of the Sacramento, California, area called *dayi*. In English, this product became known as salmon flour, and peoples across the North American salmon coasts (as well as a surprising number of cultures inland) utilized it as the base for a host of foods. Salmon flour usually began with less fatty fish from runs later in the season. The fish would be caught and sun dried, or sometimes baked, until the moisture was removed. It was then pounded or rubbed into a fine meal that kept all winter, often in underground pits or large baskets lined with maple leaves or dried salmon skin. Mixed with dried salmon roe and pine nuts, salmon flour represented one of the principal winter foods of the Wintu. Grace McKibbin, a member of that tribe, recalled that her people spent an entire week every autumn making salmon flour. Native Americans on the Columbia River Plateau added the ingredient to soups and stews. They also combined it with crushed berries, using the resulting concoction as a food source when they travelled across their countries in search of game. (Russians made a similar type of substance, grating dried salmon into soups and stews.)

Across the North Pacific, the Ainu, the great salmon eaters of the western Pacific, smoked and dried salmon to harness the nutritional value from the astounding runs of their country. As one nineteenth-century British explorer commented:

> In the season the salmon rivers were full of fish, so much so indeed that in some places they crowded one another out of the water on to the banks, and the otters and bears had glorious times among them.

Of course, the Ainu had a glorious time of it, too. Among the Ainu, the salmon were called *chipe*, translated simply as 'food', or 'the food we eat', testifying to the importance of salmon as a culinary resource and mirroring the importance of salmon to the Yurok thousands of miles away from Ainu strongholds. Although often shunned by modern consumers in the West for their lack of fat, keta and masu salmon were an especially important food to the Ainu. Keta salmon, in fact, were called *chipe kamui hcep*, or 'grand food divine fish'. These salmon and their spawning grounds dictated much of Ainu cosmology, settlement patterns and even architecture. Ainu dwellings, for instance, performed the dual role of human shelter and smokehouse. The roofs of their huts had openings at the tops of one or both of the angles, where keta could be dried for later consumption. In addition to rooftop smoking, the Ainu also preserved salmon on open-air drying frames and through

Traditional Ainu home and smokehouse.

a series of less sophisticated apparatuses made of sticks lodged in the ground.

The primary outcome of this process of smoking and drying was a product called *sake*, a dried form of *kom* and masu that was such a staple of the Ainu diet that the Japanese adopted it during the Edo period. With this foodstuff, the Ainu built an elaborate set of recipes that allowed them to live, when runs were good, with relative abundance all winter. They cooked *sake* with garlic or *Anemone flaccida*, a local flower. They also made a *sake*-seaweed soup which they ate so often that many visitors to their region considered it their primary food. 'Their food consists chiefly of dried fish, boiled with sea-weed, and mixed with a little oil made from the liver of the sun-fish', wrote a late eighteenth-century British visitor to the Ainu. Keta caught in later runs in December acquired a different taste and texture and were often made into *ruibe*, a frozen-preserved fish.

On the other side of the world, a host of novel storage and preservation techniques for Atlantic salmon birthed a variety of ɔods, many of which are better known than *sake*-seaweed soup and *chil xook*. With little doubt, the two most popular dishes to emerge form this culinary milieu were kippered salmon and gravlax. Emerging from the great runs in the rivers of Scotland, kippered salmon became one of the most widely accepted preserved marine foods in all of Europe. Called by one nineteenth-century observer 'an excellent Scottish relish for breakfast', kippered fish's earlier history hardly portended such widespread adoption. Early uses of kipper salmon or kippered salmon referred to spawned out fish that were so close to death that they were useless as human food. Throughout the seventeenth century, the term kipper referred to lean, nearly inedible fish at the end of their lives. The term, in other words, was synonymous with a fish unfit to be taken. Sometime during the eighteenth century, someone along one of the great Scottish salmon-producing rivers like the Dee or Tay made a magical leap and turned a seemingly inedible substance into something palatable. It is easy to imagine that much of humanity's culinary history involved figuring out creative ways to eat things. Mouldy cheeses, unassuming and often inaccessible grains, gnarly and seemingly inedible roots, and poisonous blowfish (*fugu*, in Japanese) all come to mind. For the spawning salmon of Scotland, this experiment began with splitting open the fish, drying and salting them, then smoking them, often over the peat so abundant in the region.

Kippered salmon became so popular that it emerged as one of the earliest important exports from Scotland, both to Britain and the European mainland. It could be used as a substitute for fresh salmon during times of scarcity, but also found its way into new culinary creations. A favourite among wealthy households in nineteenth-century France and Britain was devilled salmon. To make this, kippered fish was rubbed with mustard, cayenne pepper, anchovies and olive oil, then

William Shiels, *Discussing a Catch of Salmon in a Scottish Fishing Lodge*, c. 1840.

placed on toast, seasoned with cayenne and pepper, and baked in a hot oven. Another popular French preparation coated the kippered salmon in 'tepid' butter and rolled the fish in Parmesan cheese before finishing the dish in a hot oven. With foods such as mustard, pepper, olive oil and anchovies only available to the elite at this time, these versions of kippered salmon were ostentatious culinary displays. Despite this fact, the quality of kippered fish was still questioned by some. As it turns out, turning a near-rotten fish into a food leaves a long cultural wake. In May 1836, James Hogwarth, a London salmon salesman, was called before the British Parliament and questioned about whether 'a large portion of the kipper salmon [was] made from foul fish?' Hogwarth responded with a punctuated 'no'. Charles Fryer's classic British text of 1883, *The Salmon Fisheries*, also tried to dispel lingering questions about kippering.

F. Barlow inu.   W. Hollar fecit

In Rivers Swift, your Salmon are great store,
where with vast nets, they often bring to Shore,

SALMO

many of them, and divers other Fish,
which when well drest, fit for A Princes dish,

Wenceslaus Hollar, *Salmon Fishing*, 17th-century British etching.

There is nothing actually unwholesome in the flesh of a spawned salmon, notwithstanding the popular prejudice to the contrary; at any rate the Parisian gastronome, who is generally supposed to have a keen appreciation of the good things of this life, enjoys his diet of kelt [spawned fish], whether kippered or slated, or left to be disguised by the resources of the culinary art.

Perhaps an even more questionable method of preservation, at least in modern eyes, came from burying salmon to preserve it, a practice often associated with Scandinavian countries. For at least the last thousand years, the ancestors of the Swedes, Danes and Norwegians have been selectively burying not only salmon but also herring and shark. The salmon has taken the famous name of gravlax (often spelled gravlaks), or 'grave salmon'. In the not too distant past, gravlax connoted the actual process of burying the salmon, while *surlax* – or sour salmon – was the product that emerged from the earth. Short-term burial, usually for less than a week, took the place of cooking, while longer-term burial changed the chemical composition of the salmon enough to preserve the food indefinitely. It turns out that the longer the salmon stayed buried under the ground, the longer it remained good. It was a win-win for medieval preservationists. Burying salmon became so popular that it emerged as a profession by the fourteenth century. The name Olafuer Gravlax appeared in the records of Jamtland, a central Norwegian province, in 1348, suggesting that salmon burying had become a profession for some who were now taking it as their surname, as was common during the period. (A Martin Surlax appeared in the annals of Stockholm in 1509.) By the nineteenth century, an increasing number of gravlax producers had begun to replace burial with a combination of dill, sugar, salt and pepper. Swedes took this substance one step further, making *laxpudding*, a baked pudding consisting of rice, milk, butter, sugar and gravlax, all served with a caper sauce.

Even though it is often seen as a Scandinavian practice, in reality the tradition of storing and preserving salmon under the ground was actually a circumpolar phenomenon. Interestingly, where oceans and rivers ran cold enough to support thriving salmon runs, their grounds were cool enough to allow controlled fermentation. The Yup'ik of Southwest Alaska, for instance, also buried salmon for later consumption. They buried the grass-wrapped heads of king salmon at the end of summer, and weeks later dug up a mash that resembled something like oatmeal. It is still made in this same way today. It is said to cause hallucinations and is considered a delicacy among many villagers. Called *k'ink'* in the native tongue, the Tlingit preserved and ate salmon heads in a similar fashion. They dug giant holes below the high tide mark, lined them with heavy stones and local skunk cabbage leaves, then placed the heads in the holes. They weighed down the entire mass with boards to allow Alaska's salty tides to roll across the mass of salmon. The Tlingit ate this product unadorned, or placed it on an open fire and barbecued the fermented mass. Gravlax itself, then, did not just experience global diffusion in the nineteenth and twentieth centuries; rather, it actually had global origins.

Before industrialization, residents along the coasts of North America, Europe and Asia utilized drying, smoking, salting and fermenting to extend nature's bounty. They sought to stop the dreaded decomposition of surfeit salmon. In the process, men and women built highly sophisticated cultures around the process of getting salmon ready to store for later use. However, preserving salmon through curing was not reserved only for preindustrial societies. As industrialization emerged as an economic and culinary force in the middle of

Salmon drying in Kodiak, Alaska, 1889.

the nineteenth century, early industrial efforts to preserve fish
blended these older techniques with the innovative machinery
and labour practices that industrialization wrought. Cured
salmon began to be mass produced and to travel across the
world in these new industrially produced forms.

The world's first commercial salmon-curing operation
with global culinary consequences occurred alongside North
America's first commercial fishery, 19 km (12 miles) southwest
of Sitka along a productive sockeye run that Russian colonists
called Ozyorsk Redoubt or Seleniye Dranishnikova. The run
spilled from Glubokoye, or 'deep lake', for parts of it sank to
depths of nearly 300 m (1,000 ft). Here, at the beginning of the
nineteenth century, these ancient forms of food preservation
helped to transform the global food economy. Several mid-
nineteenth-century reports suggest that upwards of 20,000
sockeye salmon were salted at Redoubt every year, and shipped

in barrels back to St Petersburg and Moscow. There, the salted Alaskan salmon was a food reserved for the nobility. Writing about the salted salmon processed at Redoubt in 1886, historian Hubert Bancroft said that it was

> so choice in its flavor that during the regime of the Russian American Co. several barrels of the salted fish were shipped each season to St Petersburg for the use of the friends of the company's officials.

Not long after the establishment of commercial curing in Alaska, the Hudson Bay Company built a commercial saltery on the Columbia River, and began shipping salted salmon to China, Japan, Australia and the eastern United States, where it too was reserved for eaters with means. By 1902, Japan had

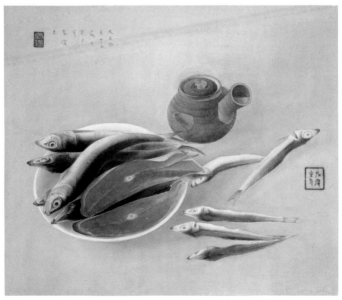

Tsuchida Bakusen, *Still-life: Salmon Slices and Sardines*, 1924.

Hanging sides of salmon after being removed from a mild cure.

established its own salteries in British Columbia, where native men and women dried salted keta salmon for export to China and Japan. By the 1930s, Japanese salteries employed hundreds of Japanese nationals and an equal number of local residents on Vancouver Island. This cured salmon was not to remain an exclusively elite food for long.

Industrial food production can be a nasty beast, but one of its beauties is its ability to cheaply mass produce foods. By the end of the nineteenth century, the infrastructure and a unique system of production were in place to allow cured salmon to begin flowing to the masses through the global food system. Much of the system was based on an initial salt cure completed near the harvest, with final processing, usually including an application of smoke, occurring in urban areas, sometimes inland or, quite often, on the other side of the globe. A significant amount of salt curing occurred across the North Pacific, for instance, before salteries shipped the fish to Germany for a final smoking. Corporations established salteries and salting houses from Yakutat in Alaska to Monterrey in California to facilitate this process. While the number of industrial salteries numbered in the hundreds on the Pacific Coast, there were also apparently a few dozen in Nova Scotia.

The salteries soon perfected one of the key elements of this transcontinental salmon network: the mild cure. For mild curing, workers immersed salmon in a brine following an initial dry salting. This immersion occurred in mammoth barrels called tierces, and represented salmon's first true integration into an industrial food chain. Invented in Portland, Oregon, in the 1890s especially for the global transportation of cured salmon, the tierces had a 360 kg (800 lb) capacity. Most of them traversed by steamship from the North Pacific to the industrial smoking operations, or smokeries, of the Eastern United States, Holland and Germany, where the salmon was finished for the markets of European nations and their imperial holdings. Although this product certainly travelled worldwide and was consumed by a host of different cultures, it eventually became closely associated with Jewish cookery. Smoked salmon sandwiches, made on rye bread and garnished with mustard and cucumber pickles, were especially popular. The mild-cured, then-smoked salmon was also made into a salad with apples, onions, roast chicken, pickled beans, cucumbers and mayonnaise, all topped with hard-boiled eggs, nuts and capers, and garnished with aspic. Another publication noted:

> it is used instead of meat, taking the place of bacon, as the thin slices are delicious served with eggs. The slices are [also] largely used as meat in sandwiches.

For most of history, salmon as a foodstuff and as an ingredient came to eaters as a dried, smoked, salted or fermented substance, especially once salmon ended their annual journeys back up their natal streams. However, a single technology emerged in the early nineteenth century that remade a salmon system which cultures around the world had crafted and sustained for millennia. It was one of the most revolutionary food inventions of all time. It remade the use and accessibility of nearly every food around the globe, and while the process of curing salmon never ended, the invention recreated salmon and the way people knew it as much as any other global food. This invention was the can.

3
Canned

The erect posture is also thought to be responsible for the
enlargement of the brain. Indeed, it is the large brain-capacity
which allows Man to live as a human being, enjoying taxes,
canned salmon, television, and the atom bomb.

G.H.R. von Koenigswald

In 1904, William Hornaday, the eminent American naturalist,
told his admiring followers that 'salmon were made for the
millions'. As a fish and a food, they had few rivals. But the best
salmon of all, according to Hornaday, was that which came in
a can. It was more than just a food, he said: it was an emblem
of American democracy and colonial might. 'In mid-ocean',
he bellowed, with a flourish typical of his style,

> the great American canned salmon is often the best and
> only fish afloat. In the jungles of the Far East, in the fron-
> tier bazaar of the enterprising Chinese trader, it 'bobs up
> serenely' to greet and cheer the lonesome white man who
> is far from home and meat markets.

Hornaday then went further:

A range of salmon cans from Alaskan canneries, late 19th and early 20th century.

> he who goes beyond the last empty salmon-tin, truly goes beyond the pale of civilization. The diffusion of know - ledge among men is not much greater than the diffusion of canned salmon.

Hornaday's salmon opus should give us pause for reasons that extend beyond the mere consumption of salmon for human fuel and nutrition. For Hornaday, canned salmon created

North America's empire by reaching into every corner of the Earth, by occupying far-flung marketplaces that sat seemingly beyond the reach of America's political, military and economic grasp, and by withstanding the toughest climates, the most inhospitable societies and the most impenetrable economies. According to the United States Department of Interior in 1916, 'canned salmon may be found in the bazaars of Cairo, Egypt, in the Streets of Jerusalem and Damascus, and in India, China, and Japan'. To a travelling American, it must have seemed like a mirage, but there it was, the can of salmon. It sat as a compelling and durable symbol of America, brought forth in a form that might seem antediluvian to us, but which in the context of the time was as cutting-edge as the car.

There was a reason for the global reach of canned salmon. Whereas curing certainly allowed salmon to be stored for later use and shipped across the globe, the processes of curing did not allow salmon to be stored indefinitely or transported easily, or exploit adequately the efficiencies and innovations of industrial production. Despite increased infrastructure and capital, curing was an antiquated process, a relic of a primal past. Canning, on the other hand, was new, innovative and efficient. It produced a food that was eminently malleable, shippable, storable and edible. Canned foods inspired respect, reverence and even awe – as they did for Hornaday. For the better part of the twentieth century, salmon *was* canned. During the halcyon days of that era, canned salmon was a staple of nearly every household in the British Empire, Europe, North America and Russia. For most, a cupboard or pantry seemed bare without a tin or two.

Any story about canning begins with a war and a dictator. During the French Revolution, Napoleon Bonaparte offered a cash prize to any citizen who could successfully invent a way to reliably preserve food. In response, Nicholas Appert, a French inventor, developed a process that took its intellectual energy from the storage of wine for later use. If wine could be sealed and preserved, why not food? Appert soon discovered that food that was heated and then sealed would not spoil as quickly as fresh food. Appert's discovery ignited a revolution, and fish were the mercenaries of this new revolutionary ideal, for even under the best conditions they spoiled quickly.

Salmon, oysters and lobster were among the first foods to be canned. Canneries that specialized in salmon multiplied along riverways that spilled into the Atlantic before arriving on the Pacific Ocean, where they also colonized the mouths of rivers with large spawning populations, much in the same way salmon did. Aberdeen in Scotland claims the world's first salmon cannery, established in 1824 at the confluence of the Dee and Don Rivers. Saint John, New Brunswick, boasted the first salmon cannery across the North Atlantic. One was built there in 1839, just above the confluence of the St John River and the Bay of Fundy. The coasts of the Atlantic hummed with the sound of salmon canneries, especially along the coasts of New Brunswick and Nova Scotia, where the Golden

Alex Brand canned pink salmon, supposedly a favourite in Scotland in the early 20th century.

Crown Canning Company of Halifax and the Northumberland Packing Company of Church Point became global leaders in salmon canning by the mid-nineteenth century. *Salmo salar* quickly became an element of a globalized food complex, part of an emerging system in which a thin piece of tin-plated iron acted as the vehicle of production, processing and transportation.

These operations on the North Atlantic coast persisted well into the twentieth century, but only as quaint antecedents of the massive enterprises that would rise along the watercourses which wound into the North Pacific. It was actually a group of salmon fishing brothers – George, John and William Hume from Maine – who teamed up with Andrew Hapgood, a pioneering lobster canner, to package that ocean's abundance of salmon into a can. They did so in 1864, along the Sacramento River in California. Hapgood, Hume and Company packed their first 2,000 cases that year. Within two years, they had expanded their operations to the Columbia

Beach seiners using horse power to move salmon from ocean to can, 1930s.

River, the great river of the American West that drained more than 570,000 sq km (220,000 sq miles) of land. At that time, the Columbia and its tributaries were the great homeland for the Pacific's *Onchorynchus*, waterways so elemental to those species that salmon's later sacrifice at the altar of industrial hydropower still mars that region's soul. Thoughts of the former abundance of salmon on the Columbia now come only in elegiac form – ballads of what once was.

The Hume Company packed 4,000 cases in its first year; still without competition, it produced 30,000 cases the following season, making it the largest salmon canner in the world. By the early 1880s, there were dozens of canneries on the Columbia River, in some years packing nearly 40 million pounds of salmon into cans, almost all of it king salmon. By the First World War, the Columbia had sent 18 million 22 kg (48 lb) cases of its salmon to every corner of the globe.

A similarly rapid expansion took place north of the continental United States in British Columbia and Alaska. In 1870, Alexander Loggie and David Hennesey built the first cannery in Delta, British Columbia, along the banks of the mighty Fraser River. Within a decade, the Fraser eclipsed all other salmon-producing waterways in Canada to become the capital of the country's salmon cannery operations. On good sockeye years – which happened every four years – the Fraser's runs challenged the Columbia's in volume. By 1900, 49 canneries stood along the banks of the Fraser alone, funnelling salmon's latent chemical energy into cans for later use by humans down the food chain.

Alaska's canneries, though, would make those of the Fraser and Columbia look as trivial and puny as their predecessors on the Atlantic. Unlike those along these two salmon rivers, Alaska's canning operations were diffused widely across the enormous territory that Russia had recently ceded to the

United States. Beginning with two small canneries in Klawock and Sitka, Alaska's canneries boomed and soon dominated world canned salmon production. By 1900, the canneries of that territory produced nearly half of the world's salmon, doubling the still massive output of the Fraser and Columbia rivers. By the mid-twentieth century, Alaska was producing nearly three-quarters of the world's canned salmon, which it shipped not only to domestic markets but also to those in Belgium, the Dutch East Indies, Mexico and the Philippines.

Alaska, the Fraser and the Columbia combined to make the North Pacific the centre of global salmon. In the 1890s, Canada and the United States controlled 99 per cent of the world's canned salmon production. Nevertheless, by the first decade of the twentieth century, Japan was slowly emerging as a player in the canning of that ocean's fish. The expansion of the canned salmon industry there happened swiftly, in large part because of the Russo-Japanese War. The war forced Japan to strive for national self-sufficiency, and the significant concessions of fishing territories made by Russia following that country's defeat certainly helped that cause. By 1930, canned salmon was the backbone of the Japanese canning industry, representing about half of all foods canned in Japan.

In just half a century, canning had eclipsed curing to become the primary means of preserving not just salmon, but all foods. After millennia of curing salmon, canning salmon ascended to its culinary throne, where it reigned for nearly a century. Even still, this transition to canning was never pre-ordained or predetermined. Commercial salteries, for one, undoubtedly eased the transition to the preservation system they preceded. These and other curing enterprises built pools of skilled and unskilled labour that knew how to deal with the peculiar nature of salmon, injected capital into regions and onto rivers; built bunk houses and factories, management buildings

Advertisement for Jubilee Brand canned sockeye salmon, featured in the magazine *Pacific Fisherman*, 1907.

and docks; and installed rail links, constructed roads, initiated water transportation and augmented marketplaces. In many ways, new canneries tied existing technologies together with new ones in order to produce immensely more efficient and productive systems. The Humes, for instance, ran a saltery for almost a decade before transitioning to canning. Alaska Salmon Packing and Fur Company's cannery at Loring, Alaska, spent years as a Tlingit fish camp before becoming a saltery. There, global salmon capital initiated the Tlingits into a system of wage labour, and soon that same capital adopted tin cans, not salt, as its primary means of preservation. The Loring cannery often led Alaska, and thus the world, in canned salmon production. (Loring, incidentally, no longer exists, even on most maps.)

In addition to the industrial jumpstart from the salteries, the improvement of canning technology itself vaulted the industry to prominence. In the early days of canning, skilled tinsmiths crafted only about 60 cans a day; by mid-century, mass production allowed one unskilled worker to oversee a machine that produced 750 cans a day. At the same time, early canners sealed each can by hand; by the 1870s, most industrial canning operations used assembly lines. The two most transformational innovations, though, were the filling machine and the automatic butcher. Invented by a Columbia River fisherman, Mathias Jensen, the filling machine replaced highly skilled and usually Chinese labour with a knife, chamber and plunger that could fill 70 cans a minute with little skilled human labour. Still, skilled Chinese workers continued to butcher and clean the salmon, and they – the lynchpins of the entire system – were the ones who ultimately controlled a cannery's productivity. They were the essential human link between nature's salmon and the global consumption of canned fish and, interestingly, with the mechanization of the rest of the process, butchers could not furnish enough cleaned salmon to keep the line operating at maximum capacity. They created a human bottleneck in a mechanical world. The introduction of the Smith Fish Cleaner in 1904 removed the bottleneck. Dubbed the 'Iron Chink', the machine could do the work of eighteen skilled men. Almost

Floating cannery, Elfin Cove, Alaska, 1940s. Floating canneries were one of the many technological innovations that allowed processors to harvest more fish.

immediately, canneries could double their capacity. Packers could keep pace with nature's abundance. In the process, the entire industry coalesced around this single technology.

This technology and mechanization dramatically lowered the cost of canned salmon, but it would be a rather remarkable marketing and branding campaign involving pink salmon that would catapult the fish to global food stardom. Through the 1890s, pink salmon, though cherished locally, was worthless on the global marketplace. The soft flesh that had evolved with the small streams of the Pacific made it virtually unusable in commercial curing operations. The common name for the fish complicated matters further: it was the humpback salmon, a translation from its Russian and scientific name, *gorbuscha*. (An easy way to remember this is to think about Soviet leader

Sockeye salmon being unloaded from a scow and taken to a waiting cannery, 1937.

Mikhail Gorbachev, whose surname stems from the same Russian root. He would be Humpbacked Michael in a literal English translation.)

Despite its liabilities in commercial curing operations, the humpback salmon's delicate flesh produced a nice canned product. It was also the world's most numerous salmon, which, in the eyes of canners, meant that it would be cheap and easy to mass produce. Its numbers, incidentally, stemmed from its natural history. *Gorbuscha* had adapted to small streams and thus had to move into the ocean much sooner after birth than other salmon species in order to find the food necessary to survive. Unlike sockeye, king and coho, all of which live in fresh water for years, humpback salmon move to the ocean after a few months. Because of the abundant marine food available to them, more young fish survived to adulthood than was the case with salmon reared in freshwater ecosystems less rich in nutrients.

In the previous preservation regime, humpback's abundance, soft flesh and funny name resulted in having little value as a food. The efficiencies and chemical processes associated with industrial canning took care of the first two hurdles. Packers in the North Pacific solved the final problem, renaming it 'pink salmon' in homage to its light-coloured flesh. They backed this linguistic act with a well-financed strategic marketing campaign. British Columbia's packers even sent a lieutenant colonel from Vancouver to England to 'undertake an educational campaign on Pink salmon'. The renamed humpback had become the canners' choice by the eve of the Second World War. In just two decades, pink salmon transformed from refuse to the king of the can. In fact, its adoption and use was one of the chief factors in the global dominance of canned salmon. The ecologies of the other six species relegated them, at least from the standpoint of volume, to a second-tier canned product, even if consumers might have preferred the taste of those species.

These combinations of events, it turns out, created a great democratic food in a century that witnessed the embrace of democracy among the world's great powers. Canned salmon was the food of the moment, a culinary talisman for citizens who wished to participate in these great social and political changes gastronomically. It endeared itself to the world and made itself an appealing part of the globe's food-ways because of its versatility, malleability, convenience and, thanks in large part to pink salmon, its price.

> It may be eaten in so many different ways that it readily adapts itself to the requirements of the breakfast, lunch-eon, dinner or supper, and gives seasonable variety to the meal,

noted a Panama Pacific International Exposition pamphlet from 1915.

> It is always ready for immediate use when the unexpected visitor happens in at meal time, or may be made to fill the most elaborate demands of a full course dinner. Canned Salmon is especially suited for picnic and outing lunches, and is invaluable for camp life.

Unlike the pronounced flavours of salted or smoked salmon, which was often used whole and broiled, baked or boiled on its own, canned salmon was more often featured among an amalgamation of ingredients, validating various claims about the food's versatility. If cured salmon was a noble food that often stood on its own, canned salmon was a melting-pot food and developed unique foodways because of it.

Its versatility as a protein made it a necessity for any pantry and the world's ultimate convenience food. The Japanese stuffed the protein into rice balls, and also made a popular tempura out of canned salmon, ginger, carrots and dried mushrooms. In Russia, canned salmon began to replace smoked and salted salmon as a popular filling for pierogi and pirozhki. A standard filling might be canned salmon, hard-cooked eggs, rice, butter and mushrooms, all tucked inside a yeast dough. Another common filling showcased onion, parsley, raw egg and canned salmon. Given their food laws, the Jewish diasporas embraced canned salmon as well. *The Complete American-Jewish Cookbook*, by the Homemakers Research Institute, featured its version of salmon loaf along with salmon soufflé, a salmon rice-ball casserole, salmon croquettes, salmon and potatoes *en casserole*, sweet and sour salmon and, perhaps most interestingly, a salmon basket: a hollowed-out loaf of bread, crusts

Loading boxes of Potlatch brand canned salmon in Petersburg, Alaska, for their trip across the globe in 1907.

removed, filled with a motley concoction of milk, bread-crumbs, canned salmon and chopped onions; the entire dish was brushed with butter and baked in a hot oven until golden-brown.

However, it would be in the homes and markets of the British Empire and the United States that canned salmon would find its most suitable home. These countries became enamoured with canned salmon not only because of its convenience, malleability, price and accessibility, but because of the role it played in both British and American conceptions of health. Britain's two most popular canned salmon producers, Pelling, Stanley & Co. and John West, both wrapped their marketing plans around claims about health, a budding interest for many consumers on both sides of the Atlantic in the early twentieth century. (In Britain, it should be noted, the decline of regional Atlantic runs spurred the sales of canned salmon from the Pacific.) In the United States, W. O. Atwater – a chemist and a founder of modern nutritional

Salmon emerged in new ways as a global food thanks to Second World War rationing and promotion programmes.

science – urged Americans to eat more salmon: it provided the nutritional punch of high-priced meats at a fraction of the cost. 'We now get, at our country grocers, 8-ounce cans of nice fresh salmon for 18 cents retail', noted a writer in the *American Agriculturalist*. 'Sirloin beef', he mused, 'costs 20 to 25 cents per lb., and pound for pound is less nutritious'. No food in the world market provided more high-quality energy for the price than canned pink salmon, and canned sockeye and king were not far behind.

Battlefields have a way of remaking cuisines, and the two major wars that the United States and Britain fought during the first half of the twentieth century also helped to popularize canned salmon in these countries and their empires. Canned salmon took a central place in the battlefield cuisine of both countries. One American publication noted that it possessed 'what it takes to satisfy the taste and body demands of vigorous, young men such as we find in the Army'. While fighting, soldiers ate salmon straight from the can and back at camp these vigorous young men satisfied the demands of their bodies for salmon in the form of cakes, hash and patties. A First World War cookbook described salmon hash made for 60 men by mixing twelve cans of salmon and 25 lb (11.3 kg) of mashed potatoes with a little beef stock, and baking the whole mixture in a slightly greased baking pan in a medium-temperature oven for just under an hour. A 1941 edition of *The Army Cook* informed its users that salmon cakes for 100 could be made easily by combining twenty 1 lb cans of salmon with 30 lb of mashed potatoes, 20 eggs and 2 lb of cracker crumbs. 'Mix well, season to taste with salt and pepper, form in three-inch cakes, roll in flour and fry in deep fat', noted the book. 'Serve hot with tomato sauce.'

The ties between war and canned salmon extended beyond the battlefield. Canned salmon was rationed less often than other meats, and governments actively promoted its consumption on the home front. 'Strange as it may seem', recalled one American,

> the taste of both liver (calves', chicken, beef) and canned salmon . . . I learned to love at a young age, thanks to rationing – it took fewer points to buy liver than the more desired cuts of meat, and canned salmon wasn't rationed at all (except during occasional shortages of cans).

These experiences cemented the British and American love affair with canned salmon. Although it might strike modern readers as odd, the fish was popular served hot or cold, straight out of the can. 'Canned salmon is delicious when eaten cold, just as it is taken from the can', according to one American author writing in the 1910s. If the cook wanted to spruce up this cylindrical curiosity, the author recommended that, 'it may be served with cold béarnaise, mayonnaise, tartare sauce, lemon juice or vinegar', or garnished with a hard-boiled egg and springs of parsley. Another typical recipe was salmon 'baked' in its own can. In this preparation, a home cook would boil her can of salmon in water for 15 minutes. While the salmon warmed, she prepared a sauce or gravy that she would then pour over the hot salmon. As one recipe explained:

> Take can from hot water; open, drain off the liquor into the gravy, arrange the fish on a platter and pour gravy over and around hot fish. Garnish with sliced lemon and parsley.

More often, however, canned salmon was mixed and moulded into other dishes. Despite an occasional baked canned salmon, it was rarely a food that stood on its own. Its culinary life depended on other ingredients, becoming dishes like salmon salad, salmon soufflé, salmon chowder and curried salmon. It also became the leading ingredient and binder in a series of dishes that included timbales, loaves, fritters, cakes, croquettes and patties. All of these dishes – ubiquitous in English-language cookbooks for three-quarters of a century – operated under one gastronomic assumption: with the addition of egg and sometimes flour (this could be actual flour, ground-up crackers or breadcrumbs), canned salmon could be moulded, shaped and flavoured into just about anything a home cook desired. Sometimes it was used with parsley, cream or mace; at other times with ketchup or onions, or perhaps a little browned butter, potato or celery salt. Rarely, however, did recipes exceed five ingredients – especially those written near the beginning of the century. Often they looked something like one of Myrtle Reed's seven styles of salmon croquette that appeared in *How to Cook Fish*, one of Reed's many cookbooks, this one published in 1913. 'Cook together one tablespoonful of butter and three tablespoonfuls of flour', she wrote.

> And one cupful of cream, and cook until thick, stirring constantly. Season with salt, red pepper, and minced parsley, take from fire, add the juice of a lemon and a can of flaked salmon. Mix thoroughly and cool. Shape into croquettes, dip in egg and crumbs, and fry in deep fat.

They also looked like one of the recipes from Van H. Tulleken's classic *The Practical Cookery Book for South Africa* (1923). Her dish for salmon fritters is both typical and instructive.

> Take 1 tin of salmon; add ½ cup breadcrumbs, 1 egg, 1 spoon finely-chopped onions, ½ spoon chopped parsley, 1½ spoon vinegar, 1 dessertspoon flour. Make into fritters; dip in egg, roll in flour, and fry in dripping.

In these dishes, the canned salmon's magnificence stemmed from its malleability, while its culinary brilliance was a result of its acquiescence to the other ingredients. As the century wore on, the additions to this trinity of canned salmon-egg-flour became more adventurous. Sour cream, green peppers, pimiento, cheeses, olives, celery, sherry, paprika, Worcestershire sauce and mustard all began to make appearances in these foods. In all of these concoctions, canned salmon subsumed the other ingredients and in the process was remade by them.

But foods, like empires, rise and fall. By the 1970s, canned salmon, like many foods before it, had lost much of its global culinary, cultural and economic value. From its peak in the 1940s, the worldwide production of canned salmon production fell significantly, in large part because of a temporary ebb in Alaska's salmon fishery. There were years in the 1940s when Alaska caught, processed and shipped well over 100 million salmon – 90 per cent of that leaving in canned form. From there, catches witnessed a steady decline, bottoming out in the 1970s at 15 per cent of the pre-war high. While it is difficult to pinpoint precisely how, when and why

King and coho salmon on deck, waiting for their trip to market.

Wild Alaska salmon fillets and steaks, ready to go into the frying pan.

canned salmon became marginalized as a great global consumer product, it is clear that by the 1970s new economic, health and culinary trends were emerging to undermine the cultural importance of this food. The global rise in both the production and consumption of canned tuna, for one, accounts in part for this decline. Canned salmon chief's gastronomic competitor, canned tuna remade the global consumption and production of canned marine products during the second half of the twentieth century. Whereas salmon might be best characterized as a global food, tuna is actually a global fish: it can be caught anywhere, not just in the colder waters that salmon need to survive and thrive. Thus developing countries such as Ivory Coast, Thailand, Ecuador, Mauritius, Ghana, Mexico and the Philippines were able to enter into both the production of tuna and the processing of canned tuna, increasing its supply and decreasing the product's cost. Benefiting from a mild taste that gave the food the sobriquet 'chicken of the sea', canned tuna sales outpaced canned salmon sales by the 1970s.

Then, in February 1982, in Brussels, Belgium, Eric Mathay and his wife sat down to a pâté made with a can of salmon imported from Ketchikan, Alaska. The meal would be one of the most important of the twentieth century. Within a week, on 7 February, the 27-year-old Belgian was dead from botulism poisoning. Revealing the interconnectedness of the world's salmon economy, it turns out that the Ketchikan can was produced for Liverpool's John West brand. (John West, incidentally, became exclusively a canned tuna brand.) John West canned salmon was at that time not only sold in Britain, but imported to the Netherlands, South Africa, Australia and, of course, Belgium. Food regulators at once mobilized to protect consumers. All five countries immediately stopped importing canned Alaskan salmon and asked consumers to discard all canned salmon packed in 1980 and 1981. Convinced that the botulism stemmed from faulty canning technology, the United States Food and Drug Administration subsequently issued the world's second largest food recall. All told, more than 50 million cans of salmon or nearly 11.4 million kg (25 million lb) from eight Alaskan canneries were recalled or discarded. Canned salmon had already become increasingly marginalized. Now it was disgraced. It reached its global nadir in 1987, when production, and presumably consumption, had diminished to about one-tenth of its mid-century heights.

However, one other force converged with the botulism scare of 1982 and the acceptance of tuna as the globe's most desired and accessible canned marine product: the tremendous growth of a worldwide market for fresh salmon, an altogether different gastronomic product from its canned counterpart. All of these events, in fact, flowed to a confluence that remade the meaning of salmon for eaters around the world.

4
Fresh

Put simply, salmon are special.

Thomas Quinn

In 1998, French chef Alain Ducasse stepped off an Alaska Airlines flight at Rocky Gutierrez International Airport in Sitka, Alaska. The chef-owner of many of Europe's most prestigious restaurants, including the renowned Le Louis xv in Monaco, Ducasse certainly seemed out of place in the frontier community. He had been hailed by his colleagues as the world's greatest chef and praised by Europe's business leaders as one of the world's greatest entrepreneurs. He was a culinary powerhouse decorated with more Michelin stars than any other living being. He had arrived in Sitka having just become the first chef in 60 years to win six stars at one time. Sitka, meanwhile, did not yet have anything resembling a decent restaurant. You might say that Ducasse was a fish out of water. However, Ducasse was not in Sitka to mingle with its culinary talents. He was there, like so many before him, for one thing: king salmon.

What Ducasse witnessed during his time in Sitka was a renaissance of sorts for an ancient fishing technique called trolling. When canning was king, catching a salmon on a

Alain Ducasse working with chefs at a cooking competition.

single hook, reeling it in individually, then processing every fish by hand – as the practice of trolling requires – made about as much economic sense as manually planting and harvesting field corn. In a system of mass harvesting and processing, speed, efficiency and volume were paramount, and fish caught by nets, in fish wheels or in fish traps provided the surest way to supply the mechanical gullets of the canneries.

In the 1980s, however, it seemed that a series of social, technological and economic developments could help save these trollers from extinction. The botulism scare destroyed Alaska's canning industry based on pink salmon and, to a lesser extent, sockeye. Conversely, however, it opened a door for those who dealt in so-called premium species like king and coho, which were usually shipped frozen or, more likely, mild cured in small shipments across the globe. New transportation innovations did not hurt either. Due to an expansion of jet service and better distribution technologies, airfreighting helped get the North Pacific's salmon to anywhere in the globe – from Tokyo and Beijing to Monaco and Paris – in 48 hours. As Ducasse explained:

> Before the advent of airfreighting in the late 1970s, the only Alaska king salmon to be found outside of Alaska waters was either smoked, canned, or frozen. Today it is enjoyed across the world.

Given these developments, it might appear that trollers should have been thriving. Yet when Ducasse arrived in Sitka, they were scrambling for their lives. Fish broker Dan Stockel solemnly recalled that 'we were just nobody', referring to their place in this new global marketplace for fresh salmon. Stockel's lament – one that he and other salmon fishermen around the globe were still trying to get a handle on – was a sign of a monumental shift in salmon production away from

Fishing boat trolling for king salmon in the North Pacific, 1930s.

Marsh Skeele, captain of the F/V *Loon*, brings on board a troll-caught king salmon.

the North Pacific and back towards the Atlantic. Whereas Pacific salmon were once the sovereigns of the can, Atlantic salmon were quickly becoming the kings of fresh fish. More importantly, these Atlantic salmon were not caught seasonally by fishermen from wood-hulled trollers, but were rather farmed in shallow-water net pens off the coasts of Norway and Scotland. There, harvested year round (by vacuum, no less), Atlantic salmon began their journeys to people's plates in the cargo holds of jets and at previously unthinkable speeds.

Aquaculture, or fish farming, turned the world's salmon production and consumption on its head. Within just a decade, inexpensive Atlantic salmon supplied by fish farms flooded the world's kitchens as the number of salmon farms exploded off the coasts of Norway, Scotland, Chile and British Columbia, allowing middle-class consumers to incorporate fresh salmon into their diets year round for the first time. Fresh salmon entered supermarkets at prices comparable to steak, pork, lamb and chicken, and found their way into cookbooks as a substitution for declining stocks of whitefish like cod and haddock. This salmon, now streaming across the globe in a raw and malleable state, transformed the way that eaters cooked and consumed salmon by linking price and accessibility to fresh fish in entirely new ways. It was a splendid new way to create and eat salmon, even though most small-boat salmon fishermen would furiously disagree.

Of course, eaters near salmon streams and along the coasts of oceans have long savoured their flesh fresh from

Fresh sockeye, lined with cream-coloured fat and ready to move from ocean to plate in ways strikingly different from those of 50 years before.

the water. However, it appears that the Chinese were the first to ship fresh fish on ice over long distances, doing so by the middle of the eighteenth century. This involved harvesting ice during winter and storing it in ice houses until needed for transportation later in the year. As for salmon, by the first decade of the nineteenth century there was an emerging, though still small, distribution network established to ship iced salmon from Scotland's salmon rivers to London. In 1816, Samuel Spiker, a traveller in Scotland, noted that iced salmon were regularly sent from the Tay to London markets. 'Each fish', he wrote,

> is packed separately in a long case, with ice above and below it; and as the smack which regularly sets sail twice every week for London, remains two days after the fish are packed up, they are covered in the meantime with fresh ice.

At about the same time, the number of commercial ice houses grew like wild flowers along Britain's salmon rivers in hopes of facilitating a domestic trade in fresh salmon with Londoners.

A similar phenomenon occurred in North America. Ice houses were built on Maine's Kennebec River to refrigerate salmon for shipment to markets on the east coast of the United States. In Alaska and the Pacific Northwest, packers such as the Booth Fisheries Company, a leader in global fisheries' distribution and sales, built cold-storage units up and down the coast for shipping small quantities of fresh salmon. However, even these refrigerated shipments almost always moved salmon that first had been cured. There was some frozen salmon, too, but when frozen and fresh salmon were combined, they remained an insignificant global food product compared with their canned counterpart. In 1917, for example, the wholesale value of all of Alaska's salmon stood at just under $47,800,000, of which roughly $46,300,000 was canned and $1,500,000 was mild-cured, dry-salted, pickled, frozen and fresh. It is thus safe to say that anything but canned and cured salmon remained rare in the global economy up through the final third of the twentieth century.

The modern beginnings of a worldwide marketplace for fresh salmon can be located quite precisely, in a fjord jutting aside the Norwegian town of Hitra in 1961. There, two brothers, Ove and Sivert Grontvedt, began catching Atlantic salmon smolts and raising them in floating net pens near their home. This seemingly inconsequential act set in motion a series of events that resulted in Norway's global dominance of the fresh salmon market. Ironically, the decline of the Atlantic salmon fishery contributed in part to this phenomenal growth. Industrial pollution, damming and overfishing had caused the collapse of the salmon fishery in the North Atlantic by the 1960s, and Norway embarked on a far-reaching fish-farming programme designed to put fishermen back to work. In essence, it encouraged fish catchers to become fish farmers by providing them with low-interest loans and state-subsidized retraining. It also limited the size of the salmon farms to encourage fair competition and low unemployment in these previously depressed fishing communities. Trygve Gjedrem, an employee at Norway's Institute of Aquaculture in Ås, expressed his enthusiasm for the project. 'Aquaculture is great for coastal development,' he trumpeted. 'For the first time, people are moving out instead of inland.'

The state support did not stop there. Norway also set up a national breeding programme for Atlantic salmon. Norwegian scientists, Gjedrem among them, were able to achieve an annual growth rate for every new cohort which

Seared salmon over spinach in a red pepper broth.

exceeded that of its predecessor by 10 per cent, or sometimes more in a good year. They also bred salmon with more fat and more resistance to disease, and salmon that showed little signs of stress when packed into cages with thousands of other fish. It had taken millions of years of evolution to create *Salmo* and *Onchorynchus*, each of which tasted of its own unique history, place and deep time. In just two generations, scientists had remade *Salmo* so completely – *Onchorynchus* was less pliant – that some began to refer to it as a new species: *Salmo domesticus*, a fish that had evolved through anthropogenic selection to the ecologies of the net pen, the dictates of production in the global marketplace and tastes contrived by human culture, now swam the Earth.

It turns out, however, that the most crucial development in Norway's industry came when the state launched its Fish

Farmers Sales Organization in 1978. The quality of fresh fish that consumers around the globe know today owes much to the formation of this organization, which spent tens of millions of dollars cooperatively marketing fresh fish on a global stage, convincing consumers, especially in targeted markets of Japan and France, that Norway's fresh salmon was a better type of salmon and a better form of food. Accustomed to the seasonality of fresh salmon (salmon, after all, are only caught when their migrations bring them back to their natal waterways), the organization undertook a sweeping credibility campaign to assure eaters that high-quality farmed Atlantic salmon could be enjoyed fresh year round. To assure this quality, the organization required exacting quality-control standards, the most stringent ever established for a marine food, and required, by law, that any salmon travelling from the country's farms met these standards. The organization enacted demanding (and then unheard of) standards for a salmon's slaughtering, cleaning, packing and handling, virtually guaranteeing a superior fresh product.

The Norwegian model, built on supplying a high-quality fresh product to consumers in Europe, Asia and North America, soon extended to Scotland, British Columbia and Chile. In Scotland, Dutch multinational Unilever created a subsidiary, Marine Harvest, to begin salmon farming operations off the Shetland Islands. By the mid-1970s, Marine Harvest was producing more than 45,000 kg (100,000 lb) of salmon a year, still a tiny amount, but enough to pique the interest of Norwegian salmon farmers, who noticed an intriguing element of Scotland's industry: it had no size limits on operations. Thanks to this, Norwegian entrepreneurs and corporations flooded the country with their capital and technology, and Scotland became the world's largest supplier of farmed

Chilean salmon farm, raising tens of thousands of salmon in a single net pen.

salmon. Unlike Norway's industry, foreign-held, multinational corporations owned almost all of Scotland's industry.

The success of salmon farming in Norway and Scotland ignited a similar industry in British Columbia. There, salmon farmers initially attempted to rear the native king and coho. They quickly discovered two problems. First, the use of endemic species increased local supplies of coho and king, and depressed the prices of both farmed and harvested fish. In the early years of fish farming, a coho was a coho, regardless of whether it was farmed or wild. Farmed king and coho, moreover, grew more slowly in net pens than *Salmo domesticus* and were also more susceptible to disease. To remedy this problem, the government of British Columbia lifted its import restriction on live roe of non-native fish, and in 1985 a shipment of live Atlantic salmon roe from Norway arrived in the province, ending a roughly 20-million-year separation between *Salmo* and the north Pacific Ocean. By 1989, there were 75 salmon farms along British Columbia's coast.

The last major player to enter the salmon-farming industry, and now arguably the most successful of them all, was Chile. The country had a series of comparative advantages that allowed it to emerge as the global salmon-farming leader by the end of the first decade of the twenty-first century. Although salmon farming was virtually non-existent in Chile in the early 1980s, the country's low labour costs, lax environmental regulations, supportive government and vast coastline convinced Japanese and Norwegian corporations to invest millions of dollars in operations there. Chile also had another advantage: there were no wild salmon with which to contend and, consequently, no possibilities of depressing local market prices for wild salmon or angering fishermen and their constituencies. However, the real advantage came in 1994, when a Chilean producer devised a cheap way to remove the salmon's pin bones, the line of sharp bones running through the middle of the fillet. Consumer friendly and easy to use, PBO – pin-bone-out – fillets became the industry standard, and only Chile had the labour costs to pursue such boning endeavours. (The pin bone removal remained semi-manual until the mid-1990s.)

After several decades of experimentation that began off Hitra, Norway, farmed Atlantic salmon, delivered fresh on demand to consumers, began to make serious headway in the global marketplace. It was an insignificant part of global salmon consumption in 1980, representing just 1 per cent of the total of salmon consumed, and only the most wild-eyed Atlantic salmon partisans could have foreseen what happened next. In the decade following, farmed salmon, symbols of a new modern food system, marched across the globe to deliver a death blow to all other forms of salmon. In 1985, the chances of eating a farmed salmon were about one in twenty; ten years later, it was one in two; by 2005, if an eater consumed five fresh salmon, in all likelihood four of those fish would have been pen reared. In parts of Western Europe and Japan, the culinary transformation was even more extraordinary. Between 1985 and 1990, for instance, the French moved almost exclusively to a diet of farmed Atlantic salmon. An eater transported to France in 1990 could expect that of eight salmon, around seven would have come from a net pen. The change was remarkable. Farmed Atlantic salmon, the fish and the food, colonized the entire globe in just one human generation (fifteen or so salmon generations, if you are counting) because of its high quality, cheap price and consumer demand.

The shift from a canned to a fresh product was equally remarkable. Canned salmon's image certainly took a bruising from the massive worldwide recall. However, more importantly, a year-round supply of fresh salmon minimized the necessity of long-term storage for a seasonal product. The beauty of canning technology was that it extended nature's

Fennel crusted fresh salmon, ready to be plated with julienned orange after a quick sear.

salmon runs through human ingenuity. Salmon in farms no longer ran anywhere. Humans could now store their salmon live and fresh in a pen rather than dead and cooked in a can. Live salmon swimming around in nets became the new warehouses for salmon storage. In the process, Gunnar Knapp, one of the world's leading salmon scholars, explained that canned salmon suffered from being old-fashioned. It was, in other words, your grandmother's salmon. Thanks to Norway's initiatives and Alaska's debacle, fresh salmon could also now claim the quality mantle, helping to drive consumer demand. In the 1980s, consumers increasingly expected food to embody quality, and fresh farmed salmon seemed best positioned to deliver that trait, creating a perfect convergence of idea and product. Although it was certainly never pre - determined, fresh salmon became synonymous with quality, and fresh salmon was almost exclusively farmed Atlantic salmon.

In this environment, authors and eaters on both sides of the Atlantic and Pacific rushed to crown fresh farmed salmon king. They mustered arguments that combined contentions about taste, laments about the ecological limits of wild salmon production and celebrations about price. In the process, they were making cultural sense of this new type of food, bringing it into their homes by telling stories that made the food more relatable. In her book *Histoire Naturelle et Morale de la Nourriture* (1987) – translated into English simply as *History of Food* – French author Maguelonne Toussaint-Samat blended all three of these points, noting that

> the looting of the salmon's feeding grounds at sea may well mean that some day the opportunity of eating wild salmon will be confined to practical experiments in historical ethnography.

She continued:

> We can at least be certain that farmed fish are a good
> species – usually Atlantic salmon – are well reared, and
> are prepared with as much care as expensive wild salmon.

In highlighting these traits in farmed salmon, Toussaint-Samat
codified all the reasons to eat this food: it was modern, tasty,
ethical and cheap.

A decade later, American cookbook author Susan Shaw
went beyond these attributes and cited freshness as the chief
reason to purchase farmed fish. 'At the moment consumers
are confused about the differences between wild and farmed
salmon', she wrote,

> but they do have a strong preference for fresh . . . salmon.
> This gives farmed salmon an advantage because it is
> difficult to supply wild Pacific salmon fresh year round.

Although such comments seem unremarkable, they clearly
reflect a new set of cultural and culinary criteria by which
salmon would be judged. By the 1990s, consumers at once
expected and exalted freshness and they knew, at least
vaguely, that farmed salmon delivered on that expectation
cheaply, consistently and, thanks in large part to Norwegian
farming reforms, with unrivalled quality.

Whereas one might expect a mid-twentieth century
cookbook to feature a half-dozen recipes for canned salmon,
by the 1990s there were entire cookbooks in French and
English dedicated solely to cooking salmon. They included
Diane Morgan's *Salmon: A Cookbook*, Bill Jones's *Salmon: The
Cookbook*, James Peterson's *Simply Salmon* from the United
States; Nick Nairn's *Top 100 Salmon Recipes*, Tessa Hayward's

The Salmon Cookbook, and Jane Bamforth's book of the same title from the UK; and Julie Schwob's *Le Saumon*, Benoit Witz's *Saumon*, and Maxine Clark's *Saumon à la carte* from France. They all featured a smattering of recipes for cured and canned versions of the fish, but make no mistake; they took their cultural energy from the 2 million metric tons of high-quality salmon streaming from the world's salmon farms and the desires of consumers to better comprehend this fresh product, found at their grocery stores year round. If art reflects life, then fresh salmon had become the new normal: of the thousands of recipes presented in these books, few, if any, call for canned salmon. Morgan's 75-recipe book, for instance, contains more recipes that call for canned chicken stock (two), than for canned salmon (none). Bill Jones's book has one lone recipe that features canned salmon, a crustless salmon quiche that combines an 8 oz can of pink salmon with skimmed milk, eggs, flour, cheddar cheese, spinach and green onions. Even the recipes for chowders, stews, cakes, loaves and soups – which would undoubtedly have called for canned salmon just a generation before – now ask for fresh fish.

THE KRASNAYA RYBA OR BLUE BACK SALMON.
Oncorhynchus nerka (Walb.), J. & G.
Drawing by H. L. Todd, from fresh fish sent to U. S. National Museum from the Columbia River, April, 1884, by A. Booth, esq.

Sockeye, the historic source of *kirimi*, an individually portioned salmon fillet found in Japan.

In Japan, a similar transformation took place. As the world's greatest salmon consumer, Japan was a unique marketplace for the introduction of the farmed fresh Atlantic salmon. Through the late 1980s, Japanese consumers sought out North American-caught sockeye as their fresh salmon of choice while still utilizing vast quantities of Japanese and Russian keta salmon for smoking, salting and drying. They preferred sockeye's bright-red colour, pungent flavour and firm texture, none of which early salmon farmers were yet able to produce. In 1989, the Norwegian Fish Farmers Sales Organization invested $10 million in a Japanese campaign to develop that marketplace and to educate consumers about the gustatory benefits of their product. The campaign paid quick dividends. Just two years before the campaign, Norwegian-farmed salmon held about 2 per cent of the fresh market; in 1991, their market share had grown to 35 per cent, where it remains, more or less, to this day. Thereafter, however, the country transitioned to Chilean farmed salmon, largely

Loading fresh salmon for the global marketplace in Seafood Producers Cooperative plant in Sitka, Alaska.

because of Japanese investments there by the Maruha Nichiro and NISSUI Corporations.

Certainly a portion of this fresh salmon made its way into *sashimi* and *nigiri*, presentations of raw salmon found at *sushi-ya*, sushi bars, and *kaiten-zushi*, larger restaurants resembling large diners. In a striking reversal of consumer tastes, Norwegian-farmed Atlantic salmon became prized in these restaurants for its high fat content and mild flavour. More often, however, the fish entered markets and homes as *kirimi*, both fresh and brined. These individually portioned salmon fillets are ubiquitous in Japan and used in a variety of dishes. Versatile and cheap, *kirimi* are central components of Japanese home cooking. They can be easily marinated in teriyaki, grilled and served over rice, shipped to work in *obento* (lunchboxes) and cooked and stuffed into *onigiri*, the omnipresent rice balls found on lunch menus across Japan.

By the late 1990s, one thing was certain: the economies of scale, the efficiencies of production, the quality of the product, the year-round availability and the ability to cut out an entire part of the food chain – the fisherman himself – allowed farmed salmon to ascend to new heights. It was, in many ways, miraculous. Workers at a fish farm off Chile's coast could wake before dawn, harvest and process fish before daybreak and have their fish on a jet liner to Paris by noon, where they would arrive that evening, to be served, seared, with beetroot, olive oil and thyme.

Meanwhile, although only about 1 per cent of the global farmed harvest made its way to consumers in a can, Alaska's salmon were still wedded to tin, a technology and preservation system that seemed hopelessly out of place when viewed against this modern backdrop. As late as the 1970s, 80 per cent of Alaska's salmon left the state cooked in tin. Even after the great botulism scare, Alaska envisioned its comeback packaged in a can, largely because it figured that it could not compete with the economies of farmed fish production in the fresh market. To lead this comeback, the state pursued a partnership with some of Alaska's most powerful fishing interests to create the Alaska Seafood Marketing Institute (ASMI), an American analogue to Norway's Fish Farmers Sales Organization. Though not totally forsaking the emerging fresh market, ASMI immediately worked to rebuild canned salmon's image with an international campaign called 'Salmon Can!' In Britain, still the world's largest consumer of canned salmon, television viewers were met with this jingle:

> What can make a salad really hard to beat?
> Salmon Can! Salmon Can!
> What can make a meal that the kids just love to eat?
> Salmon Can! Salmon Can!

Through the 1980s, ASMI continued to promote salmon burgers, spreads, salads and loaves made from canned salmon. Much as before, consumers were inundated with claims about salmon's health and cost, but this time they were also deluged with messages about its quality and how the consumption of canned salmon could help people become physically fit. The ASMI even started a school-lunch campaign and tried to hawk excess supplies to developing countries by partnering with the U.S. State Department's Food Aid programme.

This once-great food could not even summon school children and the global poor to the dinner table. Prices remained depressed for all Pacific salmon, and inventories of canned salmon continued to accumulate. Then, in 1988, Alaska's producers began a small, though concerted campaign to compete with farmed fresh salmon in France. Farmed Atlantic salmon had decimated that market for all salmon products from Alaska. Through a series of experimentations with new processing technologies – I heard one fish broker longingly reminisce about the use of machetes – and improved airfreight, a growing number of processors began moving their best product fresh into France. To differentiate this product, ASMI ran a series of advertisements about Alaska's wild salmon. 'Alaska', one read, 'was the home of good wild people.' It featured salmon-faced men and women prancing on the tops of plates. Alaska's salmon, in other words, were wild salmon and Alaskans were the Earth's great wild people. Knowing that French consumers understood the importance of quality and that Alaska's fresh salmon could never compete with farmed fish on price, ASMI used these advertisements to build the case that wildness equalled quality. Wildness, at least in this view, was as much a quality to be consumed as a state of nature. The response to the advertisements was overwhelming: ASMI was on to something. By 1991, the advertising campaign had gone global, and Alaska pursued an all-out advertising blitz that tied its salmon to the wildness of the state. To this day, consumer surveys conducted worldwide flesh this out: 'wild Alaskan salmon' is a single phrase to most consumers and exerts a tremendous amount of loyalty in those who believe in the power of wild foods.

It would, however, take more than just a high-powered marketing campaign to make salmon wild. Fearful about its possible consequences to their industry, two Alaskan legislators from Sitka, Ben Grussendorf and Dick Eliason, sought to ban all fish farming in the state. Their proposal seemed apostasy to many. The *Anchorage Daily News* called their move 'the most blatant example of using political power to protect the pocketbooks of a special interest group' the state had ever seen. Grussendorf and Eliason were currently witnessing

Wild Alaskan king salmon, painted with butter and cooked on a cedar plank.

Fresh sockeye from Alaska's Copper River at Pike Place Public Market, Seattle, Washington.

the devastation of British Columbia's fishing economy by aquaculture and justified their legislation by claiming that they were protecting the state's family fishermen, especially those participating in the emerging fresh market for king and coho salmon. After a three-year fight, HB 432 passed the State House in 1990 and with it Alaska forever banned fish farms. The bill was meant originally to protect fishermen and coastal ecologies, but its more important legacy stemmed from the fact that, when combined with the industry's campaigns, consumers would always know that Alaskan salmon would be synonymous with wild salmon.

Around the globe, the synonymy between wildness and quality – some of it real, some of it perceived – gained real traction in the 1990s, growing, incidentally, alongside an increasing amount of wild salmon entering the fresh marketplace to compete directly with farmed fish. One Canadian eater, participating in a taste test between fresh wild Pacific and farmed Atlantic salmon, noted that the wild Pacific salmon embodied 'the wild, raw taste of freedom'. Another invoked the artificiality of the farming process to construct a better tasting wild salmon. 'As with chicken', the author wrote,

> things will get better, even if the cook will have to work harder to bring this about; the fact is that farmed salmon has about it all the excitement of taste you would associate with a test-tube fish.

New York Times and *Vogue* food critic Jeffrey Steingarten went even further: 'No one should want farmed salmon', he wrote. 'It's the kind of surprise that you get when the doctor says you have herpes.'

Ironically, however, the success of wild salmon advo - cates in linking quality with the taste of their fish rested on the stupendous advances in the food system made by the fish-farming industry decades before. Not only were they borrowing much of that industry's technology, but, more crucially, they were exploiting the links between freshness and quality that fish farmers had worked so hard to establish. Simultaneously, salmon fishermen, marketers and processors used wild salmon's higher price as a way to demarcate that quality to consumers. It was a perfect fit. In so doing, fresh wild salmon slowly took its place in the modern world as a high-end niche food.

Along with this support for wild salmon, a spate of good news came in the 1990s and 2000s in the form of bad news about fish farming. During this period, consumers and environmental groups latched onto a series of scientific studies to attack industry practices. They broadcast several scientific studies that questioned the industry's use of antibiotics needed to produce the salmon in such dense environments. They pounced on a 2004 report published in the prestigious journal *Science*, which indicated that PCBs contaminated the meat of farmed salmon and that no more than 225 g (8 oz) should be eaten in any given month. They also publicized the ecological destruction associated with sea-lice infestation in net pens, and bay and inlet pollution caused by salmon waste. For many eaters, this bad publicity worked to sever farmed salmon's relationship to quality and, however unwittingly, the consumer and environmental groups that packaged and publicized these scientific findings became surrogates for wild salmon's return to the top of the human food chain.

Herein lie the context and the importance of Alain Ducasse's trip to Southeast Alaska. When he arrived, unbeknownst to the fishermen who were still struggling economically, wild Alaskan salmon shipped fresh across the globe were beginning to make their culinary comeback. Due in large part to

Unloading troll-caught salmon in California.

Wild Alaskan king salmon, just pulled from 130 feet below the boat deck.

Grilled wild Alaskan coho salmon presented with pineapple salsa.

their wild identity and farmed salmon's public relations troubles, a new and growing group of chefs, restaurateurs and elite consumers latched onto these fish as symbolic markers of quality, and in the process used them as another ingredient in the building of a new avant-garde and elite global food culture. These 'foodies', for lack of a better term, viewed Alaskan troll-caught king salmon shipped thousands of miles across the globe as a perfect expression of their food values. Trolling for salmon, to be sure, was an extremely inefficient and labour-intensive way of catching fish, but the inefficiencies became another way to construct quality, especially once these were translated into price.

In answering the call of the wild, eaters who chose to grill wild salmon over an open flame or poach it in white wine fanned the flames of food elitism. Salmon farming had not only brought fresh salmon to consumers year round, but did so at anywhere between a quarter and half the price of its wild counterpart. To question the beauties of farmed salmon, largely on merits of taste, quality or its negative environmental consequences, was to engage in the highest form of snobbery and self-centred gourmandism. 'For the time being', wrote French food author Maguelonne Toussaint-Samat, with no attempt to hide her contempt,

> prosperous gourmets claim that there is as much difference between wild and farmed salmon as between a partridge and a battery chicken. Food snobbery has been with us since Roman times.

The author had a point. Plenty of scientific research had urged consumers to reconsider their negative perception of farmed salmon: study after study suggested that the health benefits of eating farmed salmon far outweighed the costs and trade-offs of its production. Little of this, however, received publicity.

Stepping back, it is striking to witness the rancour in the debates over the merits of farmed and wild salmon. Like it or not, the battles over these fish have now transcended calories, taste and nutrition; they now represent proxies for divergent ways of thinking about food and its ties to one's lifestyle. These food fights are even more remarkable when put into a broader historical context. After all, these fresh foods have matured into a product whose recent origins as a canned good are now barely recognizable.

What makes the global emergence of fresh salmon so stunning is not just the tremendous technological, social and cultural change in the food system that the fish's flesh represents. It is also the fact that the trend towards fresh salmon offers a gastronomic reversal of other preservation regimes. Whereas curing and canning preserved salmon by removing essential parts of its nature – by cooking salmon and hiding it behind a wall of tin or by coagulating its proteins inside barrels of brine – this new system brings something decidedly more natural to consumers. Technology, in this case, has returned us closer to nature's food, not removed us from it. Perhaps it is the power that nature holds over all our cultures that makes these new debates over salmon so bitter and acrimonious. When fish is fresh, we can envision its streams and habitat, its body and its beauty. We can see it shimmer in the ocean's depths and course up streams. Nature's salmon is something worth fighting over – or, better yet, it is something to chew on.

Epilogue: The Future of Edible Salmon

Most of the world won't notice or care what happens to the
people who make their living from wild salmon.

Gunnar Knapp

When salmon becomes a food a funny thing happens along
the way. Those very traits that make it such a charismatic
creature in nature are spun, whirled and repacked to better
conform to the whimsical desires of distant markets, chimeri-
cal cultures, regional identities or finicky eaters. The way my
food community in Sitka does this, for instance, contrasts
starkly with the actions towards salmon of my other food
community, one that is 4,830 km (3,000 miles) away from Alaska
in a prairie city in the American Midwest, where I spend part of
the year teaching. The values and rituals that Sitkans nurture
to turn salmon into something edible seem foreign, perhaps
even foolish, to those in America's breadbasket. Very few
Midwesterners know the carnal joy of ritually prancing
around a boat deck in celebration of the season's first king
salmon, nor can they feel or conjure the labour of catching
and canning coolers-full of pink salmon in midsummer when
they hear that unmistakable suck from a jar of home-canned
salmon cracking open at Christmas. These are the things that

Brown sugar sockeye, cooked in a remote cabin deep in the heart of the Alaskan wilderness.

give food its cultural import. They are the processes that let humans remake nature's salmon.

Still, no matter where one is in the world, there remains something decidedly comprehensible about these different cultural processes. We are all humans, after all. Even industrial developments like Mathias Jensen's invention of a filling machine and Trygve Gjedrem's innovative breeding programmes make sense in this cultural arithmetic. These developments plunged nature's salmon into global marketplaces, and in turn churned out new types of food for the world's cultures to make their own, perhaps with rituals that are unknown to me, but just as silly as boat-deck ballets.

Less comprehensible is a development that will surely have as great an effect on the future of salmon eating as anything that has come before it. Since the 1980s, scientists have been trying to genetically engineer faster-growing salmon. Unlike innovations from scientists like Gjedrem, whose work relied on salmon's natural sexual reproduction to pass along entire genetic packages, these scientists have relied on laboratory experiments to pass along the gene or two that triggers growth in salmon. For about 3.5 billion years, life has relied on sex to pass along genes and the traits they produced. About three decades ago, scientists learned how to do this in laboratories, and there are now dozens of genetically modified plants that are commercially available to grow and eat in many parts of the world. As yet, no genetically modified animal has been made available to consumers, but salmon are by far the closest.

The AquAdvantage Salmon, trademarked by AquaBounty Technologies of Boston, Massachusetts, is that salmon. The AquAdvantage Salmon is *Salmo domesticus* with a gene sequence from both a king salmon and an ocean pout (an eel-like creature), resulting in a salmon capable of reaching a consumer's plate in half the time of a normal farmed fish. Consumers could be enjoying grilled salmon just eight months after an AquAdvantage Salmon egg's fertilization, a time period that would allow a king salmon in nature to grow to the size of someone's index finger. Despite widespread opposition from concerned citizens, the AquAdvantage Salmon is close to approval by the United States Food and Drug Administration. The global regulatory acceptance of this fish that will almost surely follow will create a protein that will fundamentally alter global food systems. It will revolutionize the way that eaters access marine foods by driving down the price of salmon – and then all fish. If their diffusion follows the arc of genetically modified plants, within a decade of its introduction AquAdvantage Salmon could represent eight out of every ten farmed salmon eaten in the world.

For eaters searching for alternatives to pork, beef, chicken or lamb, AquAdvantage Salmon will create a consumer's paradise that will make the abundance created by salmon farming appear merely mortal. More cookbooks will feature farmed salmon, more grocery stores will carry farmed salmon and more eaters, especially those in developing countries, will enjoy the taste of fresh salmon year round. Entirely new foodways will develop from this food, ones that will mirror those from farmed fish, but extend beyond them because of this new salmon's culinary and economic accessibility. From a nutritional and dietary perspective, the outcome will be equally positive. AquAdvantage Salmon will provide tens of millions of eaters with a package of proteins and fats that, calorie for calorie, will provide more nutritional benefits than any meat available for the price. This much we know.

On the other side of the globe in Sitka, Alaska, the place Alain Ducasse calls 'Salmon's Kingdom', the emergence of new foodways and food systems catalysed by AquAdvantage Salmon will have far-reaching consequences, few of them positive. Global salmon prices will plummet and so too will

Salmon boats docked at the end of a day's fishing in Sitka, Alaska.

Sunset in Sitka, Alaska.

the incentive to expend labour in stalking a fish whose value hardly reimburses fishermen for their time. Some might argue that it is actually better to let this archaic form of harvest go the way of the steam-powered locomotive and to allow wild fish stocks to recover. What they do not realize is that the very nature of wild salmon, and indeed its meaning to humans, hinge upon a global desire to consume the fish. Without this desire, the political will to protect salmon habitat crashes, the willingness to provide viable management solutions to complex scientific problems diminishes, and the cultural power of wild salmon goes the way of the salteries. With it goes all the magic that comes with knowing the taste of a fresh wild salmon beyond the immediate coasts. In other words, the entire system collapses upon itself like a gastronomic black hole, only to be rebuilt anew with an entirely differ-ent fish that respects neither nature's grand design nor the thousands of years of culinary coevolution between human and salmon.

With the global introduction of AquAdvantage Salmon, the future of edible salmon, it seems, might itself need preservation, but not in salt, smoke or tin. The future of edible salmon may need preservation in time, a type of preservation that respects the unique history and relationship among two of Earth's most remarkable beings, a relationship that the AquAdvantage Salmon threatens to unmake. In so doing, eaters, chefs, home cooks, regulators, scientists and bureaucrats will be required to reckon with whether they want to sustain a food system that supports salmon's kingdom or build one that creates a consumer's paradise, however artificial and divorced from the past. There are certainly similarities between these two futures, but a fundamental difference lies in how we treat human and non-human actors up and down the food chain. By embracing salmon's kingdom, we choose to respect and revere the miraculous natural history of a fish and the ecosystems it supports, the hard work and heritage of salmon fishing cultures across the globe, and the food special enough to deserve to be something more than a laboratory creation raised in wholly artificial environments. These are the things that should be preserved in time, and with them a taste that will connect the world's eaters to the beauty and pleasure of something larger than their own desires.

Recipes

Historical Recipes

Cured Salmon

Salmon Egg Cheese
Recorded among the Lummi by Albert Reagan,
for the Kansas Academy of Science, 1919

Place salmon eggs in a hair-seal pouch. Hang up in smokehouse
to dry and cure.

Danish Cured Salmon
From *Koge Bog* (Copenhagen, 1616)

To cure salmon, cut the back out of a fresh salmon. Put the same
salmon into a trough and spread it on both sides with blood on
the places the back is cut off. Thereafter pour salt over and under
the salmon. Let him lie in it for two or three nights depending on
how thick and big it is. Then he is hung in a room where the wind
can blow in both sides and the sun in the meantime can shine.
When the salmon has hung some time and you notice the fat
falling to the one end that's down, then you should turn it upside
down. Because if quickly smoked the salmon soon isn't good.

Swedish Gravlax (not buried)

From Sophia Lindahl, *Fullständigaste Svensk-Amerikansk Kokbok*
(Chicago, IL, 1897)

Select the best kind of salmon, shiny in the skin, the meat of a strong red color, and medium size, or from seven to ten pounds. Wash and wipe it, cut away the head and the tail; split the middle piece from the back, following the back bone as close as possible. Bone the middle pieces well, cut them in two parts each and wipe them on linen, but do not rinse. Mix a tablespoonful of pounded saltpeter, four spoons of sugar, and 1½ ounce salt, and then rub the mixture well into the salmon, after that put the pieces with their meaty sides to each other in a tub, the bottom of which is sprinkled with coarse salt and fresh dill. A cover with a weight on is now to be placed on the salmon, while the tub is covered with branches of spruce or something similar; then place the tub in a cool room or on ice, thus to remain for at least 24 hours, when it is ready. It might be taken up and used after 12 hours, but the fact is that it becomes better for standing longer. It is served in long, broad slices with the skin left on, and they are garnished with fresh dill. Eaten with oil, vinegar, pepper and sugar.

Potted Salmon

From Isabella Beeton, *Mrs Beeton's Book of Household Management*
(London, 1861)

Skin the Salmon and clean it thoroughly by wiping with a cloth (water would spoil it); cut it into square pieces, which rub with salt; let them remain till thoroughly drained, then lay them in a dish with mace, cloves, and bay leaves, and bake. When quite done, drain them from the gravy, press into pots for use, and, when cold, pour over it clarified butter.

Casolettes de Saumon

From Edith Clarke, *High-class Cookery Recipes* (London, 1885)

Quarter of a pound pastry
Quarter of a pound of Kippered Salmon
Two tablespoonfuls of Chutney
French and English Mustard
Half a pint of Aspic Jelly

Roll the paste thinly and line six oval tin dariole moulds. Fill these with raw rice, and bake. When done, remove the rice and let the pastry cases get cold. Cut the salmon into six thin slices. On each slice put a little chutney, some French and English mustard. Then roll up the slices of salmon, wrap each in greased paper, and bake about ten minutes. Remove the papers and let the fish get cold. Place a roll of salmon in each pastry case. Melt the aspic jelly, and pour sufficient over the fish to cover it. When set, it is ready to serve.

Canned Salmon

Salmon Salad

From Olive M. Hulse, *Two Hundred Recipes for Making Salads: With Thirty Recipes for Dressings and Sauces* (Chicago, IL, 1911)

Line the salad dish with two crisp heads of lettuce arranged with the darker leaves outside and the lighter ones inside. Take a can of salmon, shred the fish into small flakes, and place in the middle of the dish on the lettuce. Season with salt and a little cayenne. Pour over one tablespoonful of vinegar, and the juice of one lemon. Set on ice for an hour to cool. When ready to serve, pour one teaspoonful of mayonnaise dressing over the fish, and sprinkle a few capers on top. Nasturtium blossoms make a pretty garnish.

Salmon Fritters

From Panama Pacific International Exposition, *Salmon Cook Book: How to Eat Canned Salmon* (San Francisco, CA, 1915)

Combine one and one-third cupfuls pastry flour, two level teaspoonfuls baking powder, one-fourth teaspoonful of salt, one egg, two-thirds of a cup of milk. Mix and sift dry ingredients, add milk gradually, then egg well beaten. Season three-fourths of a cup of minced Salmon with salt, Cayenne pepper and lemon juice if desired. Add to the batter and drop by spoonfuls into deep fat and brown. Drain on brown paper, and serve hot with Tartar Sauce.

Salmon Croquettes

From Myrtle Reed, *How to Cook Fish* (Chicago, IL, 1913)

Cook together one tablespoonful of butter and three tablespoonfuls of flour. Add one cupful of cream, and cook until thick, stirring constantly. Season with salt, red pepper, and minced parsley, take from the fire, add the juice of a lemon and a can of flaked salmon. Mix thoroughly and cool. Shape into croquettes, dip in egg and crumbs, and fry in deep fat.

Salmon Patties

From Vera Van De Voort, Author's grandmother, 1960s

Combine one can of pink salmon with a quarter cup of ketchup, one egg, and one package of crushed crackers. Season with salt and pepper. Shape mixture into patties the size of your palm. In hot vegetable oil, cook the patties on both sides until brown. Serve with more ketchup, preferably Heinz.

Salmon Loaf

From Miss Tillie Brown, *Ann Arbor Cook Book* (Ann Arbor, MD, 1899)

One can salmon, 4 eggs beaten light, ½ cup bread crumbs rolled
fine, 4 tablespoonfuls of melted butter. Add the butter to the fish
and stir to a smooth paste. Beat the eggs and bread crumbs
together, then stir in the fish. Put in baking dish or mould and steam
1 hour. For sauce: One cup of boiling milk, thicken with 1 tablespoonful cornstarch, add 2 tablespoonfuls butter or oil from the
salmon, little salt, pinch cayenne pepper. Cook 1 minute and add 1
egg beaten light the last thing, pour over the loaf ready for the table.

Canned Salmon, In Can

From Carrie Etta Dwelle, *Mrs Dwelle's Cook Book: A Manual of Practical
Recipes* (St Louis, MO, 1911)

Canned salmon may be simply heated and used as the main dish for
a luncheon or Friday dinner. After it is properly heated, turn on a
dish, cover with Sauce Hollandaise, garnish with lemon and parsley.

Salmon Pudding

From Estelle Woods Wilcox, *The New Practical Housekeeping*
(Minneapolis, MN, 1890)

Chop a can of preserved salmon or an equal amount of cold,
either roast or boiled, and rub it in a mortar, or in a bowl with the
back of a spoon, adding four tablespoons melted – not hot – butter, until it is a smooth paste. Beat a half cup fine bread-crumbs
with four eggs and season with salt, pepper and minced parsley,
and mix all together. Put into a buttered pudding mold and boil
or steam one hour. Make a sauce with one cup milk thickened with
tablespoon corn-starch, the liquor from the canned salmon, and
tablespoon butter, or double the quantity of butter when the liquor
is not used, teaspoon anchovy, mushroom or tomato catsup, a
pinch of mace or cayenne, and a beaten egg stirred in last very

carefully. Boil one minute, and when the salmon is turned from the mold pour the sauce over it. Cut in slices at table. A very nice supper dish.

Modern Recipes

Fresh Salmon

Fennel-encrusted Coho Salmon with Orange Salsa

450 g (1 lb) fresh coho salmon fillet (or farm-raised Atlantic salmon fillet)
3 tablespoons fennel seed, course ground
salt and fresh-cracked black pepper
olive oil

Orange Salsa
1 small orange, seeds removed, roughly chopped
½ small red onion, minced
1 tablespoon lime juice
1 tablespoon chopped coriander (cilantro)
1 tablespoon olive oil
1 teaspoon minced garlic

Mix together the ingredients for the orange salsa. Season liberally with salt and pepper. Refrigerate for at least 1 hour (up to 24 hours). Cut the salmon fillet into four equal pieces. Season the fillet portions on all sides with salt and pepper. Press the ground fennel seed onto all sides of the fillets. Sear the fillets for 4 minutes, skin side up, over a medium-high heat in a non-stick pan, coated in a few tablespoons of olive oil. Flip over the fillet slices and cook for 4 more minutes. Remove the fillets from the pan and garnish each portion with a quarter of the salsa. Serve with a small salad. *Serves 4*

Soy and Basil Sockeye Salmon

450 g (1 lb) fresh sockeye salmon fillet
2 tablespoons brown sugar

Marinade:
1 cup (240 ml) soy sauce
¼ cup (45 g) brown sugar
¼ cup (40 g) basil, chiffonade
2 tablespoons minced garlic
2 tablespoons minced ginger
1 tablespoon sesame oil

Mix together the ingredients for the marinade and pour over the sockeye filet. Refrigerate overnight. When ready to cook, preheat the oven to 200 °C/400 °F. Place the marinated fillet on a wire rack over a baking sheet. Bake for 10 minutes. Remove the fillet from the oven and turn the oven setting to as high as it will go. Brush the excess marinade onto the fillet and sprinkle the 2 tablespoons of brown sugar over the top of the fillet. Cook the fillet for 5–7 more minutes. Serve over steamed white rice.
Serves 4

Poached Atlantic Salmon with Caper Vinaigrette

450 g (1 lb) fresh Atlantic salmon fillet

Caper Vinaigrette:
1 tablespoon Dijon mustard
1 tablespoon lemon juice
2 tablespoons chopped shallots
2 tablespoons chopped capers
¼ cup (60 ml) red wine vinegar
½ cup (120 ml) olive oil
10 cherry tomatoes, halved

1 tablespoon chopped Italian parsley
salt and pepper

Bring 2 quarters (2 l) of salted water to just below a simmer in a 4 quart (4 l) chicken fryer (or other deep-sided frying pan). Cut the salmon filet into four equal pieces, and gently submerge in the simmering water. Poaching the salmon should take 12–18 minutes, depending on the thickness of the fish and the desired doneness. While the salmon poaches, whisk together the mustard, lemon juice, shallots, capers and vinegar. Slowly drizzle in the olive oil. Stir in the cherry tomatoes and chopped parsley, and season with salt and pepper to taste. Liberally spoon the vinaigrette over the salmon. Serve with potatoes roasted in duck fat.
Serves 4

Seared King Salmon with Mustard Crème Fraîche
From Marsh Skeele, Captain of the F/V *Loon*

450 g (1 lb) fresh king salmon, preferably troll-caught from
Southeast Alaska
1 stick (110 g) butter
¼ cup (60 ml) olive oil
salt and pepper

Mustard Crème Fraiche:
¼ cup (60 ml) crème fraîche
2 tablespoons wholegrain mustard

For the mustard créme fraîche, mix together the crème fraîche and mustard, then set aside. Cut the salmon into four equal-size portions. Sprinkle liberally with salt and pepper. Gently melt the butter over a low heat, then brush it generously over the skinless sides of the salmon portions. Once the butter cools, a butter 'crust' should form on the salmon. Heat a cast-iron frying pan over a medium-high heat, and pour in the olive oil. Place the salmon skin side up in the frying pan. Cook for 4 minutes on each side. King salmon should be cooked medium rare. Serve with the mustard crème fraîche and with cooked lentils. This is an Alaskan take on a classic French preparation.

Serves 4

Select Bibliography

Arnold, David, *The Fisherman's Frontier: People and Salmon in Southeast Alaska* (Seattle, WA, 2008)

Augerot, Xanthippe, *Atlas of Pacific Salmon: The First Map-based Status Assessment of Salmon in the North Pacific* (Berkeley, CA, 2005)

Coates, Peter, *Salmon* (London, 2006)

Greenberg, Paul, *Four Fish: The Future of the Last Wild Food* (New York, 2010)

Greenhaigh, Macolm and Roderick Sutterby, *Atlantic Salmon: An Illustrated Natural History* (Mechanicsburg, PA, 2005)

Gulick, Amy, *Salmon in the Trees: Life in Alaska's Tongass Rain Forest* (Seattle, WA, 2010)

House, Freeman, *Totem Salmon: Life Lessons from Another Species* (Boston, MA, 2000)

Knapp, Gunnar, Cathy Roheim and James Anderson, *The Great Salmon Run; Competition Between Wild and Farmed Salmon* (Washington, DC, 2007)

Lichatowich, Jim, *Salmon Without Rivers: A History of the Pacific Salmon Crisis* (Washington, DC, 2001)

Montgomery, David, *King of Fish: The Thousand-Year Run of Salmon* (New York, 2005)

Quinn, Thomas, *The Behavior and Ecology of Pacific Salmon and Trout* (Seattle, WA, 2004)

Roche, Judith and Meg McHutchison, *First Fish First People: Salmon Tales of the North Pacific Rim* (Seattle, WA, 2003)

Taylor, Joseph, *Making Salmon: An Environmental History of the Northwest Fisheries Crisis* (Seattle, WA, 1999)

Walker, Brett, *The Conquest of Ainu Lands: Ecology and Culture in Japanese Expansion, 1590–1800* (Berkeley, CA, 2001)

Websites and Associations

Alaska Seafood Marketing Institute
www.alaskaseafood.org

Atlantic Salmon Conservation Foundation
www.salmonconservation.ca

British Columbia Salmon Farmers Association
www.salmonfarmers.org

Salmon Protection and Watershed Network
www.spawnusa.org

Salmon and Trout Association
www.salmon-trout.org

Save Our Wild Salmon
www.wildsalmon.org

Sitka Salmon Shares
www.sitkasalmonshares.com

Seafood Producers Cooperative
www.spcsales.com

Taku River Reds
www.takurr.net

Acknowledgements

Food is about community, and I have been lucky enough to have a wonderful one surrounding me while undertaking this project. My Sitka community helped to introduce me to the true meaning and beauty of salmon. Thanks to them all, but especially to Tachi Sopow, Marsh Skeele, Elizabeth Cockrell, Scott Harris, Andrew Thoms, Trista Patterson, Adam Andis, Jim Seeland, Justin Overdebest, Tracy Gagnon, Lexi Fish, Amelia Budd, Jeff Farvor, Ellen Frankenstein, Spencer Severson and Craig Shoemaker – all of whom, in their own small ways, helped me to understand better what makes salmon so special. Beyond Sitka, Helen Schnoes was the perfect research assistant and editor. I hope one day to be as smart and hardworking as her. The Food Over Food Literary and Culinary Society at Knox College provided an invigorating sounding board for many of these ideas, and Knox College catered to my every whim during the project. Thanks especially to Peter Schwartzman, who became a wild salmon convert during the writing of this book, and Larry Breitborde and the Andrew Mellon Foundation for their financial support for this research. Neil Prendergast has been the best of friends on all of our intellectual journeys. Few people in the profession give more thoughtful advice than Neil. Zia Brucaya is my king salmon, though. She has been patient, kind and loving through this whole process. I know you love Tombstone, but I know you love salmon even more. This book and the many feasts that follow are all for you!

Photo Acknowledgements

The author and the publishers wish to express their thanks to the below sources of illustrative material and/or permission to reproduce it.

Courtesy of Alaska State Museum, Juneau: pp. 52, 53 (photos Sara Boesser); photo JodyAnn/BigStockPhoto; p. 6; author's own collection: pp. 13, 15, 19, 71, 76, 77, 92 (bottom), 95 (bottom), 96; courtesy of Willa Brucaya: p. 36; courtesy of Molly Casperson: p. 92 (top); courtesy of Bruno Cordioli: p. 74; courtesy of Ellen Frankenstein: p. 80; courtesy of Ben Hamilton: p. 103; courtesy of Gunnar Knapp, University of Alaska Anchorage: p. 82; courtesy of the Lilly Library, Indiana University, Bloomington, Indiana: p. 9; courtesy of David Manzeske: p. 84; courtesy of NOAA National Marine Fisheries Service: pp. 25, 27, 28, 32, 46, 48, 56, 61, 62, 65, 66, 70, 75, 87, 95 (top); courtesy of James Paulson, *Daily Sitka Sentinel*: p. 88; from *Popular Science Monthly*, (1888): p. 39; courtesy of the Sitka Conservation Society: pp. 8 (photo Adam Andis), 11 (photo Matt Dolkas), 16, 34, 100 (photos Bethany Goodrich); University of Washington Libraries, Digital Collections: p. 59; Wiki-Commons: pp. 22, 55.

Index

italic numbers refer to illustrations; **bold** to recipes